Cornerstone

David A. Drown

*To Mary Beth & Tim —
Blessings!

Dave Drown*

PublishAmerica
Baltimore

© 2005 by David A. Drown.
All rights reserved. No part of this book may be reproduced, stored in a retrieval system or transmitted in any form or by any means without the prior written permission of the publishers, except by a reviewer who may quote brief passages in a review to be printed in a newspaper, magazine or journal.

First printing

Scripture taken from *THE NEW AMERICAN STANDARD BIBLE®*, Copyright © 1960, 1962, 1963, 1968, 1971, 1972, 1973, 1975, 1977, 1995 by The Lockman Foundation. Used by permission.

ISBN: 1-4137-5389-2
PUBLISHED BY PUBLISHAMERICA, LLLP
www.publishamerica.com
Baltimore

Printed in the United States of America

*For my Mom and Dad, who gave me the love of reading.
For Katie and Kevin, who both said I could do this.
For my Heavenly Father, who has blessed me with so many gifts.
And especially for my Penny...*

...my greatest gift.

Chapter 1

"Hey, good morning, Logansport. It's a little after seven in the morning. Time to finish that last cup of coffee and get out the door. This, as always, is Dan Driscoll, here for the next eight hours on Logansport, Illinois', very own, WLGP AM-610. Friends, when I bought this little station four years ago, it was supposed to be my retirement, know what I mean? That HELP WANTED sign has hung in this window for so long, you all must think it's painted on. So somebody come on down and fill out an application, will ya? I can't keep doing two shifts every day, even though I love this business.

"I understand I need to take a little longer with the news this morning as most of you in the Elm Street area didn't get your *Logansport Lookouts* today. Myrna Fielding called and said her bike had a flat tire when she went out to the garage this morning, so she's real sorry for everyone's inconvenience. She'll stop by Ernie Wilson's Ben Franklin and pick up an inner tube right after she cashes her Social Security check.

"So let's see what old Ted Friendling and the folks at the *Lookout* have for us today. There's a front-page story about the school tax referendum, and Superintendent Young has a long list of needs he'd like to implement over at the high school. There's a little item here about the tractor that caught on fire out on Cedar Road last week; Jerry King still has no idea what caused his FarmAll to suddenly go up in smoke, but it looks like he'll be taking a trip to the Cat dealer over in Pembroke pretty soon.

"Finally, here's another appeal from Father Bob Oliver over at St. Mary's. As most of you know, the building is falling down around them, so they've got this massive restoration push going, but it's tough. The estimates that have come in to restore the historic landmark are nearly a half-million bucks; if Father Bob can get pledges and donations for at least half of that, he says here he's sure the diocese won't close down the parish and sell the property.

"I think it would be a real shame, folks, if that beautiful church were let go. Most of your grandparents probably had a hand in building her back in 1921, so c'mon, dig a little deeper, will ya? Father Bob would sure like to keep his job.

"Okay, let's open the paper and see what specials are on tap this week over at Ernie Wilson's Ben Franklin, right after this word from Piggly Wiggly…"

Chapter 2

The mall was about as crowded as it usually gets on a sunny autumn Saturday afternoon. The El Encanto Heights megaplex sat snugly in the elbow of the California 101 and Glen Annie Road, just west of Santa Barbara. It was also just two miles from the beach, and on a beautiful day like today, most of the target audience would be spreading on the SPF-30 right about now. An aging Lincoln Town Car eased into a space near the main entrance. The driver shifted into PARK and let the car idle with the air conditioning at full blast. He cursed at the sunlight, knowing that inside the mall they would find mostly a battalion of senior citizen mall walkers escaping the heat, teenagers with ultra-baggy pants somehow clinging to their hips and headphones with cords leading to CD players somewhere deep in their pockets. Billy wasn't going to like this, he could tell instantly, but he wanted bookings and this was the best they could do.

"Uh, Billy," the driver said a little louder than usual. He checked the rearview mirror for signs of life. Nothing stirred in the back seat. *Nuts*, he muttered to himself. *Hour and a half drive and he's dead to the world.* He leaned backward over the seat until he was within a foot of his dozing passenger. "Mr. Delaney, your table is ready!" he shouted. Still no movement. He grabbed his front section of the LA Times with his left hand and heaved it into the back seat. The paper fanned out as it flew, and the pages spread and settled on top of a dozing William F. "Billy" Delaney, former child actor and star of the once-popular sitcom *Where's Billy?* Now, with newsprint covering most of him, Billy's driver couldn't help but recognize the irony;

Billy looked, for all the world, like the homeless sleeping on benches they had passed on the way to the mall. If his career didn't pick up soon, Billy could be joining them.

Where's Billy had been off the air for nearly ten years now. You could still catch reruns on Nick at Nite, but the suits in programming were pushing the show later and later as viewers began to dwindle. It was only a matter of time before the entire package of 118 shows would be sold to some syndicate group, who in turn would deal the reruns to a few dozen small, low-frequency stations around the country. It would provide Billy with some residual income, but he had long ago signed away most of his future royalties to his parents. That was before Max Duncan came on the scene.

Having failed to get a response with the newspaper, Max put his index finger on the little picture of the horn on the steering wheel. "Don't make me do it, Billy," he said, giving him one last chance. Nothing. *Fine,* Max thought, *it's your headache.* He leaned on the horn and watched the rearview mirror. Five seconds into the blast, pages from the newspaper flew in every direction as Billy bolted upright. Unfortunately, he forgot where he was and tried to stand up, catching the top of his head squarely on the trim between the roof and the back window.

Billy plopped into the center of the rear seat, and grabbed the top of his head with both hands. Max let off of the horn.

"Holy cripes, Max, why'd you do that?" Billy leaned forward. "Am I bleeding?"

"Look, Billy, I'm not sitting out here and baking in the sun while you catch up on your beauty sleep. Besides, I'll bet you've got a few fans inside waiting to meet you. And no, you're not bleeding. Not yet, anyway, but if you don't get moving, I may take drastic action."

"You know, Maxie, if it was anybody else, you'd be out on your can for talking to me like that." Billy slid across the leather to the car door as Max opened it for him. "But since you're my uncle, my agent and my best friend…"

"Yeah, yeah, kid, you're giving me one more chance. I'm touched. C'mon, let's go inside. Billy Delaney keeps no one waiting!" Max secretly hoped someone *would* be waiting for him.

* * *

Just as Max had feared, the half-empty parking lot spelled few shoppers inside the megaplex. Max pushed open the inner doors to the mall, and a rush of cool air greeted their faces. Two seniors, probably husband and wife, were advancing on them, more than likely on their third or fourth trip around the mall. The husband's remaining wisps of white hair flipped up as he labored to keep up with his wife, who was pumping her arms and breathing in rhythm as she kept two steps ahead of him. The man was dressed in an old blue golf shirt and polyester shorts, which revealed knobby knees and vertical scars on either side, maybe from his younger days of playing football, but more than likely because of the extra pounds he carried under his golf shirt. His wife had apparently spent more than a few minutes getting ready that morning. From the top, she sported a terry headband, although the curls of her tinted hair peaked over it in perfect alignment. She was, of course, in full makeup, looking ready for an evening on the town. She had on a white t-shirt with the picture of a dog's skeleton, along with the words "In Dog Years, I'd Be Dead." Her spandex walking pants had more span than dex, *but bless her; she was trying*, thought Max.

Max put his arm out in front of Billy as the two mall walkers went past. Billy, usually oblivious to much of his surroundings, would have stepped right in front of them. Max's arm stuck out instinctively, having prevented such mishaps on more than one occasion. Once, he had stopped Billy from walking off an observation deck during an appearance in New York City. Billy was watching a plane go overhead at the time, and Max had grabbed Billy's belt at the last moment as Billy's arms started making dual helicopter motions. "Thanks, Max," Billy had said. "Where would I be without you?"

"Probably bouncing down Fifth Avenue right about now," Max had replied. He hadn't taken Billy to any more rooftops since.

Max noticed a sign propped up against a trashcan a few feet inside the doors. It read "Come to our Center Food Court today from 11-1 and meet Billy Delaney, former star of *Where's Billy?* and get a coupon for a hot pretzel courtesy of Patty's Pretzel Palace." Max saw that someone had missed the trashcan with the last of their Orange Julius, and a streak went down the left side of the sign, ending in a puddle on the green slate floor.

"Hey, Max, maybe we can get a pretzel!" Billy gave that thumbs up sign he used to give at the end of every episode of *Where's Billy?* after he had somehow wriggled out of whatever trouble he had gotten into that week. Ten years ago, it was sort of cute when he did it in public. Now, it was just another reminder of Billy's fading popularity. It wasn't that Billy had not tried to land other roles after his show was cancelled. He went on dozens of auditions, but casting agents feared a cute kid star whose voice had changed would distract their audience. He pulled in a few guest shots on other series as some version of his old character; there was even talk of a two hour movie reunion of the show, but nothing ever materialized. Jana Baxter, who played Billy's mother, Gloria, had gone back to doing stage work, vowing never to work in television again, ". . . especially with that dunderhead Billy Delaney!" Randy Stewart, who played Uncle Teddy in the series (there was no father–single parent families were all the rage on TV at that time) had put on fifty pounds and was working at a Ford dealership in Encino. He hadn't invested well, either, unless you call betting trifectas investing.

Now, ten years later, Billy was on the personal appearance tour, but only through the efforts of Max. No one ever called asking Billy to appear. It was always Max calling the shopping malls and community centers and Little League openers.

"Billy, put your thumb down, you look like Roger Ebert's illegitimate son."

"Aw, Maxie, what's the matter, good kid?" Billy put his hand on Max's shoulder.

Even if you had a clue, I don't think you'd get it, thought Max. It wasn't that Billy was stupid; he was just, well, blissfully in his own little world, safe and secure from the pressures of common sense. In the four years that Billy acted on television, from ages 8 to12, he had very little contact with the real world. His parents saw to that. By the time Max had come into his life, Billy had little or no social skills and no friends to speak of. Now, at age 22, Max feared Billy would always need someone around grabbing that belt at the edge of life's rooftop. Max himself had just turned 68, and the gray under his cap reminded him daily that he was on the downhill side of things. He didn't know if he wanted to spend his last years babysitting Billy.

"It's nothing, Billy. Look, there's the autograph stand over there. Are you ready?"

"Ready as ever. C'mon, Maxie, I'll race you!" Billy broke into a sprint toward the autograph stand. Max watched the kid run down the center court steps to the little booth. An oversized publicity photo of Billy at age 12 was pasted to the front. Billy waved his hand to the few people sitting on the benches in the court, and plopped himself down on the stool.

No one came over to the booth. Max sighed, and walked into the Bresler's for a cone. It would be a long two hours.

Chapter 3

"Margaret Kelly?" The nurse poked her head across the counter into the waiting room and looked back and forth, waiting for someone to acknowledge.

Maggi looked left and right as well. She was the only one in the room, and wondered just how long Nurse Billings had worked in the office. "Um, I'm Margaret–Maggi–Kelly," she said as she raised her hand. The nurse looked over the top of her half-glasses at Maggi, and back down at the chart in her hand. Even though Maggi had seen the doctor at least a dozen times over her twenty years, Nurse Billings always treated her like a stranger.

"Fine, fine, Margaret. Sorry to make you wait. Come on back, the doctor can see you now."

Considering that Maggi had been sitting in the ancient lobby for almost half an hour without anyone else coming into the office, she wondered if Dr. Billings had finally finished his lunch. And maybe a nap. "Please, call me Maggi, Mrs. Billings, everyone else does." She stood up and walked towards the window. "That's Maggi with no "e" on the end. I dropped it along with my last boyfriend. You know, the whole fresh start thing, etc. My father wasn't real thrilled, but then…" Maggi noticed that Mrs. Billings had returned to her antique leather office chair behind the IBM Selectric III and the little black fan that oscillated with a quiet hum, blowing the corners up on stacks of papers on her desk. Computer technology hadn't arrived in this office and, if Nurse Billings had anything to say about it, never would.

Maggi stood patiently next to the desk as the nurse pressed a button on a brown box next to the typewriter. "Dr. Billings, your next patient has finally arrived." Maggi just rolled her eyes as her rear end still felt the impression of the 1960's orange plastic chair.

"Thanks, Mom," came the reply from the next room. "Come on in, Maggi."

Nurse Billings let up on the button, turned halfway to Maggi and said, "Right through that door, Margaret."

"Why, thank you, Mrs. Billings, and may I say it's been a pleasure meeting you. Again." The nurse may have been old, but she wasn't senile, and caught the sarcasm just as it was intended. She swiveled her chair back to the desk, and with a "Humph!" picked up a *Good Housekeeping* magazine. Maggi smiled and walked into the doctor's office.

* * *

Dr. Billings' office was on the second floor of the old Schwarz and Kelly Building on Lincoln Street, just off Main in downtown Logansport, Illinois. The brown midwestern limestone building still bore the names of its original owners along with the date of its completion, 1917, in an engraved frieze just above the main entrance. Gerhard Schwarz and Seamus Kelly were two of Logansport's founding fathers, having located their grain and feed corn-processing plant on the edge of town in 1912. The grain elevator still stood out on Route 47, but had been closed for years; a victim of Gerhard's adopted son Karl and his unwillingness to take over his stepfather's position in the company. Gerhard had never married; in 1932 he had learned of a baby boy being abandoned at the Illinois Central train station in Kankakee. Pulling a few strings, Gerhard was given custody, and plans were soon in place for Karl's apprenticeship.

Unfortunately, as Karl grew he developed a reputation as the school bully; his relationship with his stepfather deteriorated as well. When Karl turned eighteen, he turned his bullying to Gerhard, who would have none of it. Before coming to blows one evening, Gerhard opened the front door of their home, handed Karl an envelope and said, "I've given you everything you've ever wanted, boy, and a few things I thought you needed. I guess I forgot to include respect. Good luck." They didn't see each other again for nine years, until Gerhard had sent word to him that he was dying. Karl rushed to his bedside, but only because he smelled inheritance.

Two days before Gerhard passed away, he sat up in his bed for the last time and motioned for Karl to lean in. "Just wanted you to know," he said, "that everything I've got is going to the town of Logansport. They made me what I am, and I'm returning the favor. I hope you'll learn this one last lesson from me, but somehow I doubt it." Karl didn't even stay for the funeral.

After landing in Chicago, Karl took a job as a busboy at a rib house on the South Side. He worked his way into the kitchen, and after a few years and a few lucky bets at Sportsman's Park, he was able to buy out the owners of the rib house. His bullying ways never left him, and as his bank account grew he was able expand into other locations, preying on restaurants in financial trouble. As the 1960's became the 1970's, he followed the trend of themed restaurants; eventually, Karl's little empire included Chinese, Italian and even Middle-Eastern restaurants.

Seamus Kelly held on as long as he could, running the grain elevator after his partner's passing. But by the time he was in his late 70s, with arthritis and failing eyesight, he was forced to close the company and move into the Logansport Senior Center. That, Maggi's father Patrick always told her, was what killed her great-grandfather. "He couldn't take sittin' in a place like that, watchin' his lifelong friends disappear one at a time," Patrick Kelly would say.

* * *

"Maggi, you're as fit as a fiddle," Dr. Billings said, making a note in her folder. "But really, if I'm to legally call these 'annual physicals,' you have to come in once a year."

"Nobody says 'fit as a fiddle' anymore, Dr. Billings. You've really got to get out of this office. And besides, Daddy doesn't have the insurance anymore." Maggi stepped down from the table, and reached for her jacket and purse.

He finished scribbling some unreadable notes in her file and looked up at Maggi, smiling. "You're right, I do need to get a life, but when I'm not in the office, I'm usually home taking care of Mom out there. She doesn't get around much like she used to, you know."

"I heard that!" came a shout from the outer office.

"Remind me to take the batteries out of her hearing aids next time, eh, Maggi?" Dr. Billings winked.

"I heard that, too!"

"So, Maggi, what have you been doing to keep yourself out of trouble? I take it you're still headin' up the kids choir at St. Mary's, eh?"

"Yeah, we practice every Saturday morning, just like always. Mrs. McFarland still plays the piano for us, just like she did when I sang in the choir. I think she played when Daddy sang in the choir."

"Probably so. Hey, how is Patrick? I don't think he's been in for a check-up in ten years."

"Oh, you know Daddy, if nothing hurts, he doesn't see any reason to look for trouble. Besides, ever since Mom… well, he's working two jobs so I can keep going to classes over at the junior college. He refuses to take out student loans."

"Your Mom was quite a lady, Maggi. We all miss her, you know." He squeezed Maggi's hand for a second, looking her in the eyes. Maggi nodded, remembering again that her Mom and Doctor Billings had dated briefly in high school, but Patrick Kelly had won the heart of the former Miss Virginia Wellman during their senior year. Maggi quickly pushed the onrushing memories back into the corners of her mind.

"Thanks, Doctor Billings. Listen, why don't you come to Mass on Sunday? The kids are singing, and since you know most of them, I think they'd get a kick out of seeing you there."

"I think I may just do that, kiddo. I hear they're starting a fundraising drive to save St. Mary's, and I guess an old sinner like me could chip in a few bucks. You don't think my presence will bring down any walls, do you?"

"I seriously doubt it. But you may give Father Bob a heart attack!" She laughed as she stepped towards the door. "Bring your mom, too, we can use all the help we can get."

Doctor Billings shook Maggi's hand. "Okay, I'll try, but I don't think Father Bob can take one more lecture about bland communion wafers or the downfall of the church since Vatican II. I may have to muzzle her."

"I heard that!"

Chapter 4

Max leaned back on the slotted bench and watched his nephew at the autograph booth. Billy Delaney had been waving at a lot of little kids the past couple of hours, but not many people had actually walked up to meet him. Every now and then, someone would step up, shake his hand and make a little small talk. Billy would sign a picture, an old publicity still from *Where's Billy?* and offer it up to the visitors, almost begging them to take it.

Billy's uncle sighed as a couple of teenage girls walked past him, freshly autographed pictures and free pretzel coupons in their hands. They whispered and giggled to each other; Max couldn't quite make out what they were saying. He smiled. *The kid's still got somethin'*, he thought. He watched the girls head for the pretzel shop next to the hot dog stand. The pretty brunette on the right stopped outside the entrance to Patty's Pretzel Palace and dropped Billy's photo in the trashcan.

"Aw, geez, Billy." Max stood up and walked over to the booth. "Whaddaya say we head out, eh, son?" Max rested his hand on Billy's shoulder. Billy held up one finger as a woman walked up to the booth along with a little boy in a red-hooded sweatshirt. His hood was up and tied tightly beneath his round little face, and with remnants of a candy bar surrounding his mouth, he looked like a Teletubby experiment gone horribly wrong.

Billy smiled at the two. "Good afternoon, ma'am. Thanks for coming by." Billy was always polite; Max had engrained that trait in him for years.

"Um, yeah, hi. Say, listen, I was wondering if you knew where the Sears is? Back-to-school shopping, you know." The kid wiped his mouth on the side of his mom's pant leg.

Billy looked at Max, who turned his back on the woman to keep from laughing. "Well," Billy said, "I think it's down at that end of the mall, but I'm not sure. There's a directory right over there, though."

The woman took her kid's hand, which had its fair share of chocolate on it, as well. "You'd think this mall would put someone in an information booth who actually knew where the stores were." She started to walk away, and then noticed the sign in front of Billy's booth.

"Say, didn't you used to be Billy Delaney? I watched that show all the time! Always getting into some sort of mess, weren't you? Just like my little Ronald, here." Little Ronald had pulled a giant bag of peanut M&M's out of his pocket, and was biting the bag to try and get it open. With a grunt and a tug, the bag split down the middle, and little candy balls cascaded all over the center court floor. As a few M&M's rolled past Max's feet, he began laughing harder, his shoulders shaking up and down.

"Uh, I'm still Billy Delaney, ma'am. They just asked me–"

"What a shame. Someone with all of your talent and money, reduced to working in an information booth at a mall. Well, a little advice–get a map and a store directory, and you'll do fine." She lifted little Ronald off of the floor and turned towards Sears. The M&M's that Ronald couldn't reach and jam in his mouth crunched under her feet. "See, Ronald, that's what happens when you don't have any real skills." Ronald had a finger lodged in his left nostril by now, oblivious to his mother.

Billy looked up at his uncle. "Okay, Max, I guess I'm ready to go now."

* * *

Billy and Max grabbed a table in the center of the food court, their free pretzels still warm in the wax paper.

"What am I supposed to do, Max? I'm beginning to get the feeling that people aren't that interested in *Where's Billy?* anymore. I guess it's been off the air too long."

Max sipped his root beer, not saying a word.

"I don't mean to sound egotistical or anything, but my show used to be pretty popular, you know? I suppose it would help to get another job on television, but you know as well as I do that unless I play some grown-up version of that cute kid, they won't even let me read for a part."

"What do you think you should do, kiddo?" Max asked.

Billy pulled a loop from his pretzel and wiped the salt into a napkin. "I guess I could get a job somewhere, but like that woman said, I really don't have any skills, do I? Besides, what would happen to you?"

"Aw, don't worry about me, Billy. I'm a nobody. I've always been a nobody, and I'll always be one. Nobodies like us just blend into the pavement, there's so many of us. But I'll tell you one thing; you've got to stop feelin' sorry for yourself even before you start. People hate whiners–especially self-absorbed whiners."

"I know, I hate talking about myself," Billy said, "but I am worried about the future. I think what I really want is a reason to get up in the morning. You know, a plan of action, some sort of deal that'll make my life worth something to someone. Heck, it would be nice to meet a girl, too. Maybe someone who couldn't care less what I used to be."

Max slammed his cup on the table, splashing root beer all over the both of them. "THAT'S IT!" he shouted.

"What? What's 'it'?" Billy demanded, wiping the soda from his cheek.

Max leaned back in the plastic chair, laughed and clenched his hands together, shaking them over his head. "Billy, you sweet, innocent kid, I think you've tripped over the answer."

Billy had never been accused of having terrific insight; this time was no different.

"I… don't follow," he said.

"Of course you don't, kiddo, but look–you wanna make a difference in someone's life, eh? Okay, let's do it. Let's find some cause that could benefit from your time and talents. All right, your time. Let's get a million miles from Hollywood, find some social project or group that needs some help, and with my connections, we'll watch the media pour in from all over. Introducing… the new Billy Delaney! Before you know it, you'll be back on the tube, or who knows, maybe the big screen. It's a no-lose proposition!"

"But, I'll really be helping somebody, right? I mean, I'm serious about doing that."

"Oh, sure, sure. The press would smell a set-up a mile away, so yeah, you'll get your hands dirty, I'll make sure of that." Max closed his eyes, his hands resting behind his head. *It's either this or Celebrity Boxing,* thought Max, *and that Brady Bunch kid would kick Billy's rear end.*

Billy chomped on the last of his pretzel, smiling and waving at the people in line for pizza.

Chapter 5

Maggi walked out of the Schwarz and Kelly Building and paused at the bronze plaque next to the oak door. She lightly brushed her hand over the raised letters of her great-grandfather's name, a habit she started as a little girl, and now did for luck every time she passed the building.

Seamus Kelly, besides having a hand in founding Logansport, was also revered in his time for his philanthropy and unselfishness. He considered everyone a friend, and everyone knew they could count on Seamus to lend a hand when needed. His legend started in late 1917. Several of the surrounding farmers that processed their crops at Schwarz and Kelly had sons over in France, carrying rifles instead of pitchforks. The older men were having trouble getting in the crops that fall, so Seamus organized a small army of his own. He went door to door in Logansport, asking if the local men could lend a few hours each week in the fields. Not a single ear of corn fell to the crows that year.

The fact that Seamus' partner Gerhard was a German immigrant didn't seem to matter to the people of Logansport. Long before the First World War, Gerhard Schwarz was instrumental in organizing the first town council. When water pipes were first laid throughout the town, it was Gerhard's math and engineering skills that helped move the project along. So when Seamus' army hit the fields that fall of 1917, Gerhard was in overalls right beside the others. No one ever questioned his loyalty or his patriotism.

Maggi turned south on Lincoln towards Main, walking past the little shops that made up the so-called business district in downtown

Logansport: Betty's Sunflower Shop, The Mane Event Hair Salon, Bill & Karen's Sporting Goods. Ernie Wilson's Ben Franklin sat at the corner of Lincoln and Main. As Maggi walked around the corner, there was Ernie in the front window, arranging a new display of school supplies. Even though the temperature had climbed over 80 that day, Ernie still wore his daily uniform of white short-sleeved shirt, buttoned to the top with a red and blue striped tie. Ernie himself had passed 80 several years ago, but no one would have ever told him to retire; he loved what he did and promised to be a display himself someday when he was gone.

Maggi rapped on the window. Ernie looked up with a jolt, his mouth open in a perfect circle of surprise. When he recognized Maggi, a huge grin crossed his face just as his upper plate dropped out of place onto his lower lip. She put her hands over her own mouth in mock surprise; Ernie was always doing that for the little kids, just to get laughs.

"Hi, Maggi!" Ernie called through the window. He waved a box of yellow Ticonderoga #2's at her. "The good old days, huh?" he shouted, pointing at the pencils.

Maggi nodded. "You bet, Ernie. Hey, I need to run, but don't you spend too much time in that hot window, okay?"

"Don't worry about me, hon. Mrs. Wilson says I'm half-baked already, so I won't be out here too much longer."

She blew him a kiss. "See you at Mass on Sunday!"

"Wouldn't miss it!"

That was a truth if there ever was one. Ernie Wilson was fond of telling everyone that he was the first baby baptized at St. Mary's after they installed the marble baptismal font in 1922, and had only missed one Sunday ever since–his honeymoon.

A few shops down the street, and Maggi found herself standing outside the old Roxy Theater. Underneath the black overhang and white art deco letters, their once white shine now yellowed, the majority of the light bulbs surrounding each letter gone or burned out. The Roxy sign could be seen in just about every downtown photo ever taken, much the same as the Chicago Theater sign is used in tourist promotions for the Windy City. The Roxy hadn't shown movies in years; in fact, the doors to the seating area had been boarded up years before. The lobby was converted to a business office almost twenty years ago. Several tenants had opened and closed a variety of businesses in that time without much success. The Roxy sat empty for almost two years until Dan Driscoll had moved to Logansport.

Dan was the type of person one notices right away, a self-proclaimed free spirit and aging baby-boomer grappling with inner conflicts he never shared with his friends. His graying hair was pulled back in a ponytail, despite his ever-retreating hairline. He wore nothing but t-shirts and jeans, and his Harley was a fixture on the downtown streets. His beard was kept short and neat, showing mostly salt with a little pepper. Dan Driscoll had left a highly successful construction business in the Chicago suburbs "to get back to the real world," as he put it. On a road trip one weekend, he checked into Bea and Al's Bed and Breakfast on Locust Street, and had stayed ever since.

Six months after checking in, he was granted an FCC license and WLGP was on the air. He rented the Roxy's offices; put his studio in the front window and a 5,000-watt transmitter on the roof. He had a deep appreciation for the old standards, filling Logansport's radios with Sinatra, Rosemary Clooney, Doris Day and Mel Torme. The kids in town laughed at the "really oldies" station, but they wore headphones attached to CD players anyway and wouldn't know good music to save their souls. Dan didn't care; he loved his adopted town and played music he felt was a nod of recognition to a lifestyle that personified the town, a way of life on the endangered list in America, a sweeter time.

As Maggi stepped over to the window, Nat "King" Cole was coming through the outdoor speaker above the door. His silky, tenor voice was reminiscing over lost love.

Dan waved at Maggi from his chair and took off his headphones. He got up and headed to the front of the window where tickets were once taken. Maggi fished through her purse, pulled out a folded piece of paper and slipped it through the half-moon opening in the glass.

This was the accepted means for getting announcements read on the air at WLGP.

Dan took the note, unfolded it and quickly scanned the writing. He signaled okay with his hand, and Maggi mouthed "Thanks" back to him. She turned and headed for home, just three blocks away on Grand Avenue. There was barely an hour before her father came home for dinner, and two hours before she met with the kids for choir practice.

Dan Driscoll plopped back down in the old leather chair behind the console and put his headphones back in place. The last few notes of the song faded; he lifted the needle from the turntable and flipped the studio mike switch to "On."

"Wasn't that a beautiful memory, everyone? That was Nat "King" Cole and 'These Foolish Things.' Well, before I dig any further in my box of dusty-musty LP's, the lovely and gracious Maggi Kelly just stopped by and wants me to remind everyone in the kid's choir from St. Mary's that you've got practice tonight at 6:30, and don't forget your music. Which reminds me, folks, Father Bob needs a couple of volunteers to come by the church on Saturday to do a little plaster repair work in the side entrance area. I've seen Father Bob's skills as a handyman, so please come on down and help him out. Just kidding, Padre. Now, let's sit back and let Peggy Lee tell us about her 'New York Blues'."

The needle found its groove, and Dan leaned back in his chair.

Chapter 6

The silver-metallic Mercedes looked out of place among the other cars parked along Canal Street. This side of Kankakee had seen better years economically, and most of the Queen Anne-style homes in the neighborhood had overgrown lawns and were in desperate need of paint and nails.

The Bishop's residence had stood in the center of the block since its completion in 1879. Century-old oak trees surrounded the large, squarish dolomitic limestone building. A half-dozen squirrels chased each other in the front yard among the newly fallen leaves. Acorns were everywhere, and occasionally one would hear a soft "pop" as an acorn landed on the flagstone path leading to the massive front doors to the residence.

Directly behind the building sat the Cathedral of St. Theresa, another beautiful limestone structure and a fixture of the Kankakee landscape. The front entrance faced Marengo Street, its bell tower soaring five stories above the golden blanket of leaves in the parking lot. At precisely two minutes before noon, the first of twelve tolls rang from the ancient lone bell atop the steeple.

Both driver and passenger in the Mercedes looked at their watches.

"Almost time, boss," said the driver.

The passenger tugged at a cufflink, a black onyx with the solid gold initials "KS" in the center. Quarter-carat diamonds bordered around each cufflink. Karl Schwarz had held many meetings in his life, but none quite as important as this one.

"All right, let's go, Jimmy."

* * *

The two men entered the large foyer of the Bishop's residence after a disembodied voice buzzed the front door open.

Jimmy Dozan turned in a slow circle as he surveyed the portraits of Kankakee's past bishops. "Man, boss, look at the size o' them pitchers."

Jimmy was a classic toady, not too bright, loyal to the bone. After dropping out of high school, his massive size led him into the Marines, but his equally large compassion for food landed him in the mess tent as a cook. After his discharge two years later, he was hired by Karl Schwarz as a broiler cook at the Steak and Stein, a new restaurant in Chicago's Hegewisch neighborhood. That was twenty years ago, and in that span Karl had opened another fifteen theme restaurants throughout the city, and Jimmy had kissed enough rump roast so that Karl would finally hire him as his personal assistant.

"Jimmy, stand still and act like you've been here before," Karl muttered.

"But I ain't been here before."

Karl grabbed Jimmy by the arm. "Just keep quiet, understand? You want the Bishop to think we're a couple of yahoos?" Karl's cold gaze over his glasses told Jimmy that Karl was serious. Dead serious.

A young priest bounded down the main staircase at the rear of the hallway. Karl noticed the priest's perfectly combed hair and his confident walk as he approached the two visitors. The young man offered his hand to Jimmy first.

"Good day, gentlemen, I'm Father Miguel Santos, the Bishop's administrative assistant." He grabbed Jimmy's hand and shook it vigorously. "You must be Karl Schwarz," he said.

Jimmy pointed his left thumb at Karl. "No, he must be Karl Schwarz." A nervous giggle popped from his throat as he looked at Karl. Father Miguel let go of Jimmy's hand quickly.

"Oh, I beg your pardon, Mr. Schwarz. Please follow me; the Bishop is ready to receive you." Father Miguel put his hand on Karl's back and guided him towards the staircase. Jimmy fell in behind the two, wishing Father Miguel cared who he was.

* * *

Father Miguel rapped lightly on the door to the Bishop's office. Without waiting for a response, he turned the crystal doorknob and poked his head inside. "Bishop Barnes, the gentlemen from Heritage Restaurants are here."

After a second, and with no audible response from the chamber, Father Miguel opened the door fully. "Please gentlemen, go in," he said.

Karl and Jimmy walked into the brightly lit room. A crimson carpet covered the oak floor, and two tallback chairs were positioned in front of the six-foot desk. An equally large leather chair faced the back of the office towards a lead-framed window. Branches from one of the oak trees waved just outside in the afternoon breeze.

"Have a seat, Mr. Schwarz," came a voice from somewhere inside the leather chair. Jimmy and Karl looked at each other, shrugged their shoulders and settled into the seats. Father Miguel sat in an armchair against the wall, picked up a notebook on the side table next to him and began scribbling a few notes.

"It's a beautiful day, isn't it?" Bishop Barnes was still facing the window. He didn't wait for a response. "You know, a lot of people have trouble with the changing of the seasons. The end of summer for so many signifies an end, a dying of sorts. And, I suppose, they're right in a way. Many things do die, or at least go dormant. I, on the other hand, prefer to look at this time of year as an opportunity to plan for the beauty of the coming spring." The leather chair swung around and faced Karl and Jimmy.

"That's why I was so interested in your proposal, Mr. Schwarz." He lightly tossed a manila folder on the desk. "But I am nothing if not a patient and thorough shepherd of my flock. I felt it only prudent to hear your offer in person; pie charts and bottom lines tend to bore me."

Karl leaned forward in his chair. "Your thoroughness is greatly appreciated, Bishop Barnes. It's the way I've always done business, and wouldn't expect anything less from those I deal with."

The Bishop placed his palms together, fingers extended. His elbows rested on the arms of the chair, and he looked as if in prayer. "Please go on. And perhaps I should inform you that we have a cleaning person in this office, so I won't need anymore sucking up."

Jimmy, already breaking out in a sweat, suddenly found this hilarious, and let out a short laugh. Karl deftly placed his right heel squarely in the center of Jimmy's left foot, and applied enough pressure to end the outburst.

"Uh, sorry, your honor," Jimmy said to the Bishop, and not knowing what else to do, made the sign of the cross.

Karl patted Jimmy's arm. "My assistant doesn't get out much." Jimmy looked down into his lap.

"As I was going to say," Karl continued, "I've been in the restaurant business for over two decades now. As you have seen in my offer, I have taken older buildings and refurbished them, creating profitable dining establishments that incorporate the original themes of the buildings. The owners of the buildings have always insisted that I maintain the original architectural integrity, as well. Here in Kankakee, for example, I created the Brass Mill Restaurant in the old Anaconda Brass Works office building. Not a stone in the structure was touched, and it has become a very popular dining spot in town."

"Yes, I've eaten there several times," said the Bishop.

"Then you of all persons can appreciate the sincerity in my proposal. It's always been a dream of mine to create a restaurant within an old church. Think of the menu possibilities! Adam and Eve apple salad, Burning Bush flambé, you get the idea…"

"I suppose I do, Mr. Schwarz. But tell me, why this particular church in this particular town?"

Karl shifted in his chair; he knew this question might come up, and was ready for it. "Because it's my hometown, Bishop. When I left so long ago, it was a strong, vibrant little town, the kind Norman Rockwell used to paint. And after I heard of the decline of the parish and the dilapidation of the church itself, I wanted to give something back and resurrect the town. I even attended Mass in that beautiful building as a boy, and couldn't bear to see it close."

"I see. All right, we'll need some time to consider your offer. I'll be meeting with the Diocesan Council at the end of the month, and will present your offer at that time. In the meantime, please wait for further word from me or Father Miguel." Bishop Barnes stood up from the leather chair, and Karl, Jimmy and Father Miguel stood as well. The Bishop extended his hand to Karl, and held it for a second with a firm grasp.

"You know, I really love the sea bass at the Brass Mill," said the Bishop.

Karl pulled a card out of his left coat pocket. "Please take this with my compliments, Bishop. Show the maitre'd this card anytime you're in the Brass Mill, and dinner's on me."

Bishop Barnes placed the card on his desk. "That's not really necessary—"

"I insist! Please, it's the least I can do for this consideration." He turned to Jimmy. "Let's let the Bishop get back to tending his flock." Jimmy stuck out his hand to the Bishop, but the Bishop had returned to his chair and was reading through the folder. Jimmy thought for a second, and snapped off a salute instead.

"Thanks, your emanation," Jimmy said. Karl grabbed Jimmy's collar and pulled him towards the door.

As Father Miguel opened the door for them, Bishop Barnes called out. "Oh, by the way, Mr. Schwarz, I meant to ask you; have you actually been back to Logansport in all these years?"

"Oh, absolutely, Bishop, many times." This was the second lie, and Karl didn't want to push his luck any further, especially in this room. He and Jimmy hustled through the door and down the stairs to the Mercedes.

Chapter 7

The Monday following the disastrous mall appearance, Max and Billy were on the road. Max convinced Billy that it would make an interesting story if the two of them set out like a modern-day Don Quixote and Sancho Panza, searching for windmills to topple and damsels to rescue.

Unfortunately, *Man of La Mancha* hadn't been on Billy's list of must-reads, but he trusted Max with his life, and the two were off with the sunrise. "We're just gonna head east," Max said, "and when we find the right project for you, we'll know it." Billy nodded in approval. For the first time in his life, Billy Delaney was feeling a different kind of tug on his sleeve. As long as he could remember, he had been led around on a short leash wherever he went. As a child actor, he had absolutely no cognizance of social issues, and his every waking moment was filled with taking direction from someone. His parents (before the court order) would wake him every day at four a.m., and after force-feeding him bran muffins and OJ, would rehearse his lines until it was time to leave for the studio.

At the studio, a cadre of stagehands, make-up artists and gophers were assigned to know the whereabouts of Billy at all times, therefore someone was always within three feet of him. During his first season, Billy had wandered off the set during a break in the shooting and had given himself a two-hour self-guided tour of the various soundstages. After a frantic search, he was found jumping up and down on the set of "The Price is Right," holding hands with one of Barker's Beauties. He was never out of anyone's sight again.

Max stepped into Billy's life halfway through the third season of

Where's Billy? A new contract for Billy had been negotiated after the network had renewed the series for a fourth year, but it was heavily laden with up-front cash that was supposed to be deposited in a trust fund for Billy. When the studio's accounting department asked for an account number, Billy's parents became elusive as to the account's actual whereabouts. This set off alarms all through the business department, because nobody wanted another messed up child star on their hands. After an investigation, it was discovered that Billy's parents had actually put the vast majority of his earnings into an offshore account in Bermuda.

The custody trial was short; Max was Billy's only living relative, his mother's brother, and was only too happy to take the young man under his roof. The money, almost $400,000, was never recovered, and Ed and Sheila Delaney left California two weeks after the trial. After twelve years, Billy never mentioned them. Max wouldn't bring them up in conversation, either, except to tell Billy that "thieves wear many masks, kiddo; you've gotta watch out for yourself. I'll watch your back." Billy appreciated Max more than even Max probably knew. And he respected him. Honesty will do that; Max never held back in laying it on the line for Billy, giving him life's little lessons from a street-wise point of view. In return, Billy had privately sworn that he would be as honest and giving as Max had been with him.

* * *

"Hey, Max, check it out." Billy was pointing at a sign a short distance up the highway. "Caroline's Choo-Choo Caboose Inn and Diner. Aw, man, we gotta eat there, Max. Maybe spend the night, too. Whaddaya say?"

"Sounds good to me, Billy. Real America, you know?"

"Right, real America."

Max turned the Lincoln onto the gravel path leading up to Caroline's. "Well, would you look at this," Max exclaimed.

Barely fifty yards from the highway sat six old railroad caboose cars. Directly in front of them was a long, silver railroad car with a neon sign flashing "DINER." A set of stairs led up to the door, and on a pole next to the steps hung a small OFFICE sign. The diner was fully lit, and an old red Chevy Cavalier was parked out front. It was the only car.

"I haven't seen any signs for restaurants lately either, Billy," said Max. "You're right; it's probably our best bet."

It was after six p.m., and the setting sun behind the Rockies had turned the early evening sky into a beautiful meld of reds and purples.

"That's the joy of this trip, Billy. You never know where you'll find your destiny. But just between you an' me, I doubt if it's gonna be in a caboose in the middle of the desert."

Max parked the Lincoln next to the Cavalier, and the two got out. They stretched for a minute before heading up the wooden stairs into the diner.

Kenny Chesney's "The Good Stuff" was coming through an old Magnavox in the corner. A middle-aged woman behind the counter looked up from her magazine at the two visitors as they settled on red plastic-cushioned silver stools in the middle of the dining car. Billy grabbed a couple of menus from behind a napkin dispenser and gave one to Max.

"Evenin', boys," the woman said, grabbing an order pad and walking over to them.

"Hi, there," said Max. "I'll bet you're Caroline of Caroline's Choo-Choos."

"And I'll bet you're hungry," she replied.

"Boy, howdy!" Billy said with a drawl.

Max and Caroline looked at Billy.

"What?" Billy said. He thought everyone talked like that out here.

Max cleared his throat. "Uh, anyway, whaddaya recommend, Caroline?"

"Besides paying in cash? Well, you can't go wrong with my pork chop sandwich. An inch thick on Western toast."

"Sounds great. Give me one of those, some fries, and a cup of coffee."

"Comin' up." She looked at Billy. "How about you, Hopalong? Beans and biscuits after a long day on the trail?"

Billy flipped over the menu. "I reckon a turkey sandwich on whole wheat, mayo on the side would do just fine, ma'am. And a glass of water, if you please." Then he took a pair of sunglasses out of his pocket, put them on and sneered, "Go ahead, make my sandwich."

Caroline laughed. "Oh, you do impressions! Can you do Clint Eastwood, too?"

Max thought this was the funniest thing he'd heard all week. "You'll have to excuse my young friend here, Caroline. You know, he's one of those show-biz types, always on."

Caroline grabbed a pork chop from the refrigerator at the end of the counter and threw it on the grill. She poured the coffee and the water and set them in front of the two. "Show business, huh? You know, I thought you looked familiar," she said as she pointed at Billy. "You used to be on television, didn't you? What was that show... oh, it'll come to me in a minute. What in the world brings you out this way?"

Billy grinned behind his designer shades. "We're on a mission from God," he said, hoping she might recognize his Elwood Blues impersonation.

"Is that so?" she said, as she tossed some French fries into a basket and set them in the deep fryer. "Gonna save the world. Well, Lord knows, the world needs savin'. So what's the plan, sheriff?"

Billy pulled off his sunglasses. "Um, that's the part we haven't figured out yet. My Uncle Max and I are looking for a cause that could use some support. I guess you could say I'm trying to find my true purpose in life, and Max is my Mario Lanza."

"Sancho Panza," said Max, winking at Caroline.

Caroline flipped the pork chop, and pulled a couple of slices of wheat bread from an orange wrapper and set them on a plate. "So you really are on a mission, aren't you? Well, good for you. I never gave much credit to you Hollywood types, always lookin' for publicity for yourselves. You guys even hold press conferences when you go into rehab, for goodness' sakes."

Max sipped his coffee. "I can assure you, my darlin' Caroline, that my nephew here has never needed rehab," he said.

"Maybe not, maybe not. But if you're truly interested in doing something good with your life, maybe you ought to be on a 'mission from God.'" She reached behind a four-slice toaster and picked up a book. She flipped a few pages through the middle, until she found the page she was looking for.

"Here, read this while I put your sandwiches together," she said.

Billy took the book from Caroline. She pointed halfway down the page. "Matthew, chapter 6, verse 2."

Billy read out loud: *"So when you give to the poor, do not sound a trumpet before you, as the hypocrites do in the synagogues and in the streets, so that they may be honored by men. Truly I say to you, they have their reward in full. But when you give to the poor, do not let your left hand know what your right hand is doing, so that you will be giving in secret; and your Father who sees what is done in secret will reward you."*

Billy looked at Max. "Sounds good to me, Uncle Max." Billy handed the book back to Caroline as she set their plates down in front of them. Max just nodded and finished his coffee.

"Thanks, Caroline, I'll try to remember this," Billy said.

"Somethin' tells me you will. You've got those honest eyes, you know?"

Billy blushed. "Aw, go on…"

"That's it!" Caroline shouted. "You were Kevin Arnold on *The Wonder Years*! I'd know you anywhere!"

Max looked at Billy. "I told you those shades wouldn't work, Billy. Pass the ketchup."

Chapter 8

"... So once again, that's black seedless grapes at forty-nine cents a pound at the Piggly Wiggly. These and other great deals are in today's Sunday *Logansport Lookout*. I'm, as always, Dan Driscoll, and if you're listening to me on WLGP AM-610, you're either getting ready for church or you're on your way.

"Tell you what, folks; drop a couple of extra coins in the plate at St. Mary's today, could ya? I have it on good authority that Father Bob's restoration fund is nowhere near what he needs in pledges to save the church. Remember, you'll be helping to preserve our history and the memories of nearly everyone here in Logansport.

"In honor of St. Mary's, here is a little Doris Day for you, reminding us that whatever will be, will be."

* * *

Dark brown oak leaves crunched under Maggi's feet as she headed east on Locust towards St. Mary's. It was almost 9, and she had promised Father Bob and the kids that they would run through the music parts of the mass one last time before the 10 o'clock service. Maggi absolutely loved being the children's choir director. She didn't have to worry about the things the adult choir often fought over– harmonies, missed rehearsals, and all the rest of the small town gossip that went on between hymns. Her kids, as she called them, loved being in the choir just as much. They were pretty good about showing up on time, memorized the words better than any adult, and whatever they lacked in tonal abilities, they made up for in enthusiasm.

As she approached the driveway to St. Mary's, she stopped for a second to look at the steeple looming above her. *This really is a beautiful old church*, she thought. The massive outer oak doors were splayed open as they always were in good weather, and Maggi could hear a few notes from the organ as Mrs. McFarland warmed up. Father Bob refused to even lock the church at night; the little town was relatively crime-free, and he saw no need to prevent anyone from finding a quiet place when they needed one.

Maggi climbed the limestone steps and stood outside the doors. No one stood in the narthex yet, but she could see a few of her kids wandering around the choir area to the left of the altar. She leaned against the hand-made red bricks just above the cornerstone with the block-style "A. D. 1921" engraved on the front and side. The day was almost too beautiful to go inside, so she promised herself a long walk after Mass. Maggi walked through the doorway, waving at Mrs. McFarland as the kids settled in their seats.

* * *

"… And so, my friends, it is with a very heavy, sad heart that I must share some news today." Father Bob Oliver was usually pretty good at hitting his seven-minute mark for homilies. Today's, however, had already stretched to ten minutes; several rear ends were already squirming in the ancient wooden pews. Father Bob seemed to stretch the homily a bit, trying to avoid this apparently painful announcement.

"The Diocese," he continued, "has informed me in writing that they have given us exactly four weeks from today to secure the pledges needed to renovate and restore St. Mary's. Bishop Barnes will come here himself and announce the decision based on what we present to him. As most of you know, we are not anywhere near our goal of $450,000. In fact, to date we have generated only about $70,000 in pledges and a little over $5,000 in cash, thanks to bake sales, car washes, and weekly donations."

Ernie Wilson sat with his wife Grace in the same pew every week in the nearly sixty years they had been married, and today was no exception. As Father Bob broke the news, Ernie turned his bowed head towards Grace. She looked at him, and they both knew that this was not good. She and Ernie had already given as much as they could spare; most of the $5,000 in cash had come from them. Selling the Ben Franklin was out of the question, and no bank would allow them to take another mortgage at their age. Grace took Ernie's hand and gave it a gentle squeeze. "They'll figure something out," she whispered. Ernie nodded his head, but deep in his heart, he wasn't so sure.

Father Bob continued. "As wonderful as bake sales and car washes are, somehow I don't think the Bishop will take them in collateral for saving the church. The purse strings are tightening all over the Diocese, and I guess we just don't rank up there very high on their priority list of expenditures. Quite frankly, friends, I'm out of ideas. With only four weeks to go, I think our last, best chance is prayer. I've asked so much of you in the past, this is all I can ask of you now." Father Bob turned and walked back to his chair. As he sat, this was Maggi's cue to begin the preparation hymn.

Maggi's kids handled the mass parts without incident, and sang a beautiful version of "One Bread, One Body" during Communion. The church was only half-full, so Communion was finished long before the end of the hymn. Mrs. McFarland held the last note for a fraction of a second longer than usual, and it echoed throughout the church as everyone sat in silence. The parishioners were a bit stunned by Father Bob's announcement, unable or unwilling to comprehend the possibility of the church closing. Mrs. McFarland sniffled at the organ, on the same bench she had occupied for over thirty years. Dr. Billings and his mother had shown up, thanks to Maggi's invitation, but were surprised at the somber mood they found themselves in.

Father Bob stood up and said, "Let us pray." The altar server walked up the four steps to the pastor, holding the Bible above his head. He read a brief passage, thanking God for every gift received, and then asked for his continued blessings and gifts as He saw fit. He closed the Bible and turned to the congregation, raising his hands.

"Now may the Lord bless you and keep you. May the Lord lift up his countenance upon you and give you peace. In the name of the Father, and of the Son, and of the Holy Spirit…" As they each made the sign of the cross, the congregation intoned, "Amen."

"Go in peace to love and serve the Lord," the Pastor finished, grasping his hands and holding them close to his alb.

"Thanks be to God," the faithful of St. Mary's responded.

This was Maggi's cue to introduce the closing hymn. She stood and turned towards the congregation; Mrs. McFarland sat up a little straighter at the ancient pipe organ, ready to play with a little more determination than usual. *It wasn't much,* she thought, *but maybe it would help inspire a few more pledges.*

"Please join us in singing 'Faith of Our Fathers,' number 600 in your hymnals." Maggi turned to the children, mouthed the word "Ready?" and nodded in Mrs. McFarland's direction. The veteran organist set the volume two notches higher, and as the first few chords from the refrain bellowed throughout St. Mary's, the vibrating pipes were hardly noticeable from the congregation. As little Meghan Vogelman squeaked the second line of the hymn, "In spite of dungeon, fire and sword," she looked up above the organ in time to see a two-foot square chunk of plaster falling earthward. Later, she said it seemed like it was falling in slow motion; she followed its path as it landed squarely on Mrs. McFarland. Powder plumed outward from the organist's general area as the music stopped. The congregation stopped singing as well, and stared unbelievingly at what was happening before them.

The church almost at once became utterly silent. Father Bob, who had been looking down at his hymnal, first looked at the congregation, wondering why everyone had stopped singing, and then followed their gaze towards Mrs. McFarland. Maggi stood frozen in mid-conducting as pieces of the plaster scattered around her feet.

Mrs. McFarland stood up from the organ bench, looked over to Father Bob, and said, "I think we should have a silent recessional today." As Maggi rushed over to her, Mrs. McFarland wobbled a bit, finally dropping to the floor as Maggi caught her under the arms. Dr. Billings half-jogged up to the organist, followed closely by Mrs.

Billings.

"Caroline, are you all right?" he asked. Mrs. McFarland nodded but didn't say anything. Maggi wiped some of the plaster powder from her face and tried to remove a few of the larger pieces from Mrs. McFarland's bee-hive hairdo, which was now much smaller than its original six-inch height. "I think she's a little stunned," Maggi offered.

The crowd around the scene had grown now. Dr. Billings asked one of the parishioners to get a glass of water.

Caroline McFarland looked up at the ceiling, and then at Maggi. "Maybe we should stick with the piano for the time being, okay?"

Chapter 9

Dinner that Sunday afternoon at the Kelly's was more quiet than usual. Maggi had taken the long walk she promised herself, but couldn't enjoy the autumn weather knowing that the church she loved would probably be closing. *Whenever two or more are gathered*, she kept thinking to herself. Why did everything have to revolve around money? The implication that churches can only function if they are profitable seemed to contradict that old Bible quotation. St. Mary's was built with sweat equity by her great-grandfather and the rest of Logansport, with the only "pledge" being that they would worship in His house forever. As she neared home, the afternoon skies had clouded over, matching her mood.

Patrick Kelly's car was in the driveway. Maggi's father had worked for nearly thirty years as a day foreman at the Austman Foam Products plant over in Morris, which manufactured car and truck seating. The Morris factory employed a third of the population of Logansport, and Patrick had been there nearly the longest. At one time, Austman had seven plants scattered across the Midwest, but downsizing and import competition had reduced the company to just the Morris facility and a smaller, satellite location in Milton, Wisconsin, just North of Rockford.

In order to save his job, Patrick had accepted more than one pay cut, despite the best efforts of the union. Then, a week before last Christmas he received a form letter in his pay envelope telling him and the other employees that health insurance premiums would now be his responsibility and would be automatically deducted from his salary. A strike was out of the question; instead, he took a second job as a weekend security guard at the Logansport Savings and Loan. It was easy work; he sat behind a desk from midnight to seven watching reruns on a portable black and white television. He didn't even carry a gun, as Logansport hadn't had an actual violent crime since someone had held up the Gas 'n Go in the late 1970's.

Maggi and Patrick made it a point to have Sunday dinner together at 3:00 every week. As she walked up the front path, she looked at her watch and realized she had been wandering around Logansport for nearly three hours after Mass. She hurried through the door, threw her purse and keys on the table and walked straight into the kitchen. She loved cooking for her father, and cherished their Sundays together. She flipped on the kitchen light, opened the refrigerator door and pulled out the chicken and rice she had made the night before. Maggi turned on the oven and set the glass pan in the center rack.

"Hi, sweet pea," Patrick said, walking into the kitchen.

She turned with a start. "Oh, hi, Daddy. I'm sorry; I didn't see you sitting in the living room." She kissed him on the cheek. "I'll have everything ready in about half an hour."

Patrick pulled out a chair from the kitchen table and sat down. "How was Mass, honey? The kids sing okay?"

"The kids sang fine, Daddy. It was the rest of the Mass that was a disaster."

Maggi set the kitchen table as she first recounted Father Bob's announcement, and then the plaster incident with Mrs. McFarland.

"You mean, right on top of the head?" Patrick asked, laughing.

"It's not funny, Daddy. She could have been hurt."

"And the dust shot out everywhere?"

"Dad!" Maggi glowered at Patrick.

"I'm sorry, honey. I'm glad she's okay, but I can just picture it ..."

"Well, anyway, I'm more worried about the diocese closing St. Mary's. Can you believe it–just because it's an old building that needs a facelift, the Bishop would throw away almost a hundred years of history over $450,000."

"Maggi, $450,000 is a little more than a facelift. But it's not like it used to be. All the hopes and prayers and wishes of the town won't make it happen, like they did when it was built. I remember your great-grandfather tellin' us how a young priest ..."

"Father Kevin Birmingham," said Maggi.

"Yeah, Father Birmingham. He was assigned by the diocese in 1908 to establish a Catholic parish here in Logansport. Then, with the help of just about everyone in town, they built that beautiful old building from scratch, right up to forging the bells in the tower. Father Birmingham and your great-grandfather loved that church, and were great friends for many years."

"I know, Daddy, and that's what makes it so sad." Maggi sat down next to her father at the kitchen table. "In my mind, that was exactly what Jesus wanted people to do–build a church with their hearts and their hands, and with faith, the rest would take care of itself. Now, though, all we ever hear about is pledges and bottom lines and maintenance costs."

Patrick reached over and took Maggi's hand. "Well, sweet pea, you've never been one to sit around and let something happen. What are you going to do about this?"

"I don't know. I've been out walking for the last three hours, trying to figure that out."

"Hmm. You know, Maggi, I don't always have many answers, but I seem to remember a daughter of mine that took a course in journalism once. In fact, she got an 'A' as I recall. How's your letter writing skills?"

"What do you mean, Daddy?"

"I'm just saying that maybe you need to spread the word about St. Mary's outside of our little town, that's all. Maybe tell her story to a few newspapers in Chicago, Springfield and Joliet. It couldn't hurt."

"I suppose you're right. Okay, I'll put something together after dinner; I think I've still got those editor's addresses from class."

"That's my girl. Now, tell me the truth–it was Caroline McFarland's hair that saved her life, wasn't it? You could bounce a two-by-four off that 'do ..."

CORNERSTONE

"You're awful!" Maggi stood up and walked over to the kitchen counter, and turned on the portable radio.

* * *

"...And that was Charlie "Bird" Parker and his alto sax with a great rendition of 'Now's the Time.' This is Dan Driscoll, and speaking of time, it's nearly 3 o'clock, time for me to head over to Bea and Al's for dinner, so while I'm out, please sit back and enjoy a few selections from Eleanora Fagan Gough, otherwise known as the great Billie Holliday."

Chapter 10

The early morning sun began to bake the inside of the caboose. Billy's right arm jutted out of the upper bunk, and as he snored, a fly settled squarely above his left eye. It walked around his entire face, pausing slightly on a trail of drool sliding down Billy's left cheek.

Perhaps it should have moved on. With one great snore, the fly disappeared down Billy's throat, only to appear seconds later as he sat bolt upright in the bunk, banging his head on the roof of the caboose and coughing at the same time. The fly shot across the room, hitting the wall before it could comprehend what had just happened, and dropped down into one of Billy's tennis shoes, dead.

"What the heck – OW!" Billy rubbed the growing knot on the top of his head, amazingly near the one he gave himself that day in the car before the shopping mall fiasco.

"Max! Hey, Maxie?" No answer. Billy jumped out of the top bunk and realized that Max had already dressed and left. He peeked through the window; the Lincoln was still in front of the diner. *Yeah, breakfast, that sounds good.* He quickly rinsed off in the closet-sized shower, shaved, dressed, and packed his bag.

* * *

"Well, if it isn't my favorite TV actor. How'd ya sleep, deputy?" Caroline poured Billy a cup of coffee as he sat down at the counter next to Max.

"Not bad. Got any Raisin Bran?"

"Sure." Caroline set a bowl in front of him along with a pitcher of milk. She grabbed the box of cereal from a shelf above the counter. "Rule here is you get as much as you want for a buck and a quarter."

Billy smiled. "Thanks, Caroline. So what were you two up to before I got here, huh? I'm not going to have to find the meaning of my life by myself, am I?"

"Naw, nothin' like that. Your uncle was just thrillin' me with all of those Hollywood stories, you know? Like the time you got bubblegum stuck in Barbara Bush's hair when she visited your set."

"Now, come on, they told me not to chew gum when she came in the room. How did I know she'd want a hug?"

"Oh, man, she was irritated," said Max. He and Caroline laughed, as Billy turned slightly red, and then laughed a little himself.

"Caroline, I'd love to keep sittin' here all day, enjoying your company, but Billy and I need to head on up the road. How about one last cup?"

She filled both mugs as Billy wolfed down the last few bites of Raisin Bran, then chugged the coffee.

"Here, Billy, I'll let you drive for a while. Throw the bags in the trunk, and I'll be outside in a minute." Max slid the car keys across the counter.

"Oh, okay, Max. I mean, OH, OKAY, MAX!" A big grin crossed his face.

"Get outta here before I smack that smile off of ya'." Billy jogged outside.

Max turned back to Caroline. "Hey, listen, thanks for taking the time to listen to an old man's troubles. I do love that kid, you know. His parents really didn't do him any favors, the way they treated him. I just want him to be happy."

"Max," Caroline said, taking his hand, "where I come from, people like you are known as guardian angels. At least you've found your lot in life. You should be proud of yourself."

"Well, I feel a little guilty, hoping to use whatever it is he decides to do to help revive his career."

"Honestly, haven't you heard a word I've said all morning? Whatever he decides to do that will make him happy–and as long as he's helping others–that's when he'll get his reward. If that means a return to television, then so be it. Just let it happen, Max."

Max looked out the window, and then back at Caroline. "Thanks, kiddo," he said.

Billy ran back into the diner and sat down in one of the booths. He pulled off his shoe and held his foot into the air towards Max and Caroline. "You guys see anything? It felt like a rock or something, but I can't find it." The recently departed fly sat squarely in the center of Billy's sock.

Chapter 11

Maggi sat down at the old Hewlett-Packard desktop and logged on to the word processing program. Patrick had turned in, and a cool breeze floated through the den as Maggi leaned back in her father's leather chair. Somewhere on the block, kids were playing Ghost in the Graveyard, and their distant laughter brought a smile to Maggi's face, and she wondered if any of them were in her choir. *You're the ones I'm doing this for,* she thought.

"To whom it may concern," she said as she typed and the words fell on a blank page. *No, too trite.*

"To whom it SHOULD concern." *That's better.*

> My name is Maggi Kelly, and I am the children's choir director of St. Mary's Church in Logansport, Illinois. I am writing today to ask for your help. You see, our wonderful old parish building is in danger of being closed by the diocese only because of some structural repairs they say need to be done. We've been given four weeks to come up with $450,000, or they will close us for good. Our little town has done everything we can to raise the money ourselves, but it's just too much.
>
> Let me tell you a little about St. Mary's. Some look at it and say what a quaint old building, pretty stained glass and all. Those of us who are members here, though, look at it and see a home, our home away from home, so to speak. Our families have

been baptized and confirmed and married here, going back three generations. We've held hands as we prayed the Lord's Prayer, and sang "Silent Night" almost in a whisper at Christmas.

And now, they want to close the only church most of us have ever known because of money. But I'm not writing this letter asking for donations. I'm writing to ask for an angel, someone who can help us help ourselves. The people of Logansport are some of the proudest folks I have ever known, but all they have left are their prayers.

I'm praying for an angel.

The words appeared quickly on Maggi's computer screen, almost as if someone was typing for her. She closed with her phone number and address, and the address of St. Mary's. As if on cue, St. Mary's bell tower rang out a single toll in the distance, signaling the bottom of the hour.

She closed her eyes. "Heavenly Father, if it is meant to be, then it is up to me and thee." She crossed herself, and fought back tears.

Maggi printed the double-spaced letter, and by the next morning fifteen different newspaper editors had received it over their fax machines.

Chapter 12

The Mercedes pulled up in front of Bea and Al's Bed and Breakfast shortly after dusk that same Sunday. The only other vehicle in sight was Dan Driscoll's Harley-Davidson parked in the gravel driveway, which wound around the back of the old Victorian home to a detached garage. In the front yard was an old sign, badly in need of paint, which read "Bea & Al's B & B" in block letters, with the words "A little taste of Cleveland" in smaller print underneath.

Bea and Al DeWerth had found Logansport twenty-some years earlier much the same way everyone else did–by accident. Recently retired, they were on an antiquing trip across the country, and knew enough that the best deals could be found in little towns off the interstate. The previous owners of the bed and breakfast, Jack and Peg Noonan, had decided to move to Arizona with Peg's brother and be rid of the snowy winters once and for all. Jack was pounding the For Sale sign in the front yard the afternoon Bea and Al pulled up front. "I told Al I wanted antiques, not an antique house," Bea would tell everyone. Within a month, they closed on the house.

But they loved the old place, and spent several years restoring the original woodwork, rewiring ancient sockets and running new plumbing throughout before they reopened the bed and breakfast. It was a labor of love; they didn't expect many guests, as Logansport didn't have much of a tourism draw. They averaged four or five overnighters a year, but always had a full dining room for their old-fashioned Sunday dinners. Dan Driscoll was their only full-time boarder, and they only agreed to that after they heard of Dan's plans for WLGP and the old-time music he was going to play. In return for their hospitality, he looked after Bea and Al, and did a little yard work for them when he had free time away from the station.

"This is it, Jimmy. There weren't no Bea and Al's here before I left town. We should be able to keep a low profile until the Bishop comes." Karl Schwarz peered out through the smoked-glass as the streetlights began to glow. "Same old ratty little town, though, ain't it, Jimmy? Somethin' tells me they could use a good restaurant around here."

Jimmy Dozan looked in the rear view mirror at his boss. "Beats me, Mr. Schwarz, I ain't never been here before."

"Howzabout you get the bags out of the trunk, and we'll check in, huh? And remember, I'm Mr. Jenkins and you're Mr. Hundley, and we're just in town for a few days on business. Nothing more than that, just business. If anyone gets nosy, tell 'em to buzz off."

"No problem, boss. I mean, Mr. Jenkins. Hey, Jenkins and Hundley, the pitcher and catcher for the Cubs in the '60's. That's good, Mr. Schwarz."

"Now, you see there, dipstick, you've blown our cover already. Don't call me Mr. Schwarz from here on out." Karl climbed out of the back of the Mercedes and headed up the path to the house.

Jimmy unloaded the trunk, and with two bags under each arm and a garment bag hanging from his collar, struggled up the same path. *Dipstick, huh?* he thought. *Maybe someday you'll find another dipstick that'll put up with your stuff, 'cause I'm sure gettin' sick of it.*

The front door banged against a little bell suspended beneath the transom as the two stepped into the parlor. "Just a minute," a voice called from upstairs as Jimmy set the bags down.

Karl looked around at the antique furnishings. "This looks like a scene out of *The Music Man*," he whispered.

"Was that on MTV, boss?"

"Oh, shut up. Here she comes."

Bea bounced down the wide staircase and walked over to the two visitors.

"Sorry, gentlemen, we were catching a little TV after dinner. How can I help you?"

"We would like to know if you have a couple of rooms available for a few days. My name is Mr. Jenkins, and this is my associate, Mr. Hundley. We're in town on business and need to stay for some time. I hope we didn't need to make reservations."

"Reservations?" Bea asked incredulously. "Well, let me check my availability." She walked over to an old leather book on a desk and flipped it open. Dust flew up as she thumbed through a few pages. "Looks like you're in luck, boys, I think I can squeeze you in." She rolled her eyes, and Karl smiled, feigning appreciation for her attempt at humor.

"Excellent," he said.

Bea pulled two keys from the same desk and handed them to Karl and Jimmy. "First two rooms at the top of the stairs on the left. The rate is thirty dollars per day including breakfast and a buffet dinner on Sunday. Sorry, you just missed that. We take most major credit cards, and don't allow smoking anywhere in the house. So how will you be taking care of the bill?"

Karl pulled a thick envelope from his jacket pocket. "We'll pay in advance. Do you still accept cash?"

Bea's eyes widened. "Oh, every now and then, we take it for old time's sake." She tucked the bills into her jeans, and turned toward the staircase. "Let me get the bellman for those bags. HEY, AL!"

"Whaddaya want, Beatrice? I'm watchin' women's softball up here."

"We have a couple of guests checking in."

"Oh? Well, the staircase is right there at the end of the hall. I doubt they'll get lost on the way to their rooms."

"They paid in cash, Al."

Before Bea could turn back to Karl and Jimmy, Al was coming down the stairs three at a time. "Hey, guys, let me get those bags. Tell you what, I've got ESPN on in the library, suds cooling in the fridge, and Beatrice here would be glad to throw a pizza in the oven, wouldn't ya, hon?" Bea nodded, and Jimmy smiled approvingly.

"Oh, gosh, that sounds like more fun than we've had all day, Al," said Karl, "but we've got an early meeting tomorrow. Maybe another time." Jimmy let out a little moan, but Karl's glance stifled any further sounds.

"All right, fellas, you name the time. C'mon, I'll show you the rooms." As the three climbed the stairs, Al shouted over his shoulder. "Hey, Beatrice, better let Dan know he needs to get back to the station."

"He's on his way, I just saw him go out the back. Good night, boys!" Beatrice called out.

The distinctive low pop pop of Dan's Harley filled the quiet night as he pulled out of the driveway and headed back to town, but not before he took note of the Mercedes. *Guests for breakfast,* he thought.

Chapter 13

Max and Billy headed east on Interstate 40 after leaving Caroline's. Max's thought was that they head somewhere into the heartland, the Midwest. "Flyover country," he called it. "That's where you'll find real people, Billy. Real people with lives and jobs and kids and mortgages and a million stories to tell."

They cruised through the Petrified National Forest into New Mexico, and continued on into the smokestack of Texas, stopping east of Amarillo for the night. No cabooses this time, though; a Holiday Inn did just fine.

The boys hit the road early, and by lunch had made it into Oklahoma City. Here, they connected onto I-44 because it headed northeast into Missouri all the way to St. Louis. From there, they would connect with I-55 all the way north to I-80, which crisscrossed the country's midsection like a belt.

By the end of the third day, the conversation had tapered off to an occasional "hey, look at that." Max insisted on driving most of the time, while Billy would read every local newspaper they picked up at every pit stop. After years of Variety, Max thought Billy could broaden his horizons just a bit.

About thirty miles outside of Springfield, Missouri, Max noticed a sign for Lambert's Café in Ozark. Ozark was a little town of 10,000 just south of Springfield, but what caught Max's eye was Lambert's slogan, "Home of the Throwed Rolls." *That sounds too funny to be true*, he thought. Max detoured the Lincoln down to Lambert's shortly after noon.

They pulled into the Lambert's entrance, and found a nearly full lot even though it was Tuesday. Billy was still deep in the Tulsa Times, reading about the worries of brush fires after an unusually dry summer.

"Hey, Max," Billy said, looking up from the newspaper. "You hungry again?"

"Aw, just look at this place, kid. Antique signs all over, a boardwalk—I'll bet we can get a great meal here. Besides, I could use a break."

"Sounds good to me, Maxie. Let's eat."

The boys walked in, and were immediately greeted with what sounded like a player piano somewhere in the restaurant. The crowd was noisy, too. Large picnic benches filled the main dining room, and servers were walking up and down the aisles with large bowls of various kinds of food. The walls were covered with old signs, posters and photographs, and as Max and Billy were escorted to a bench, they noticed the piano along the wall, and behind it a bluish white-haired head (hopefully attached to an elderly woman) bobbing up and down to the music as she banged out some long-forgotten rag.

The kitchen door swung open with a loud bang and a server pushed a cart loaded with dinner rolls out into the main aisle.

"Roll!" he shouted, and a couple of hands went up in the restaurant.

Max and Billy watched in stunned amazement as the waiter picked up a handful of rolls and, with Kerry Wood accuracy, pitched a roll into each of the raised hands.

"Max, did you see that?"

"How could I miss it? That last one went right over my head. I guess that's what they mean by 'Home of the Throwed Rolls.'"

"I sure hope they throw one to us, huh?"

"I think everyone gets one. What are you gonna eat, kiddo?"

They studied the menu for a few minutes, the shout of "Roll" coming from behind them every so often. A server finally took their order, and ran off to the kitchen.

"Listen, Billy, I've been thinkin'. Ever since we left L.A., you seem like a different kid."

"Whaddaya mean, Max?"

"Well, for one thing, you don't talk about yourself so much, so you're a lot quieter. You're not having second thoughts about this, are you?"

Billy looked around the room at all the different diners in Lambert's. A couple of truck drivers in one booth, laughing in their conversation. A group of moms and little kids filled a whole picnic bench. A young high school-aged couple, probably skipping school, sat by the window.

"Max, do you see these people?" Billy said in almost a whisper. "They've got lives, responsibilities, people who depend on them for what they do. They'll probably spend most of their lives no more than twenty miles from where they were born, and no one outside of the little towns they were born in will ever even know they existed. And look at them. They're happy, Max. They're smiling and laughing and enjoying each other's company. And then there's me."

"What about you, Billy?"

"Exactly, Max, what about me? What have I ever done besides focus everything on me? I must be the most self-centered person anyone's ever known. Billy Delaney, former child star. Well, big whoop-de-do."

"Roll!"

"Aw, Billy, don't worry about–"

A roll sailed the length of the dining room to the high school boy near the window, who caught it with one hand.

"I'm so helpless and self-centered, I've got my uncle drivin' me around trying to find myself."

"Wait a minute, kid, this was my idea. We're gonna get you back on track, just you wait and see."

"Yeah, right, we'll see, Max. I know we need the income, but…" his voice trailed off.

"Hey, don't you worry about money, and don't you worry about me. You just worry about gettin' happy. All right?"

Billy nodded, but that sparkle in his smile was nowhere to be seen.

"Roll!"

Max raised his hand, and Billy half lifted his arm above his shoulder. The first roll found Max's fist perfectly, and a few diners applauded, as was the apparent custom. Billy's throwed roll was a good foot and a half from Billy's hand, when he suddenly sneezed, jerking his hand down into a fist in front of his face. The incoming roll glanced off of the bald head of a businessman seated directly behind Billy and landed on the table of the two truckers. A rousing chorus of boos arose, along with the two truckers, who stepped over to Max and Billy's booth, the fresh, warm roll in one of the men's hands.

"I believe this is yours," said the trucker. He handed it to Billy, and resting both fists on their table, leaned into Billy and said, "Yer allowed t'drop one, buddy. Drop two, and y'gotta eat 'em both no matter where they land. Be glad we caught this'n for ya." With that, the two truckers roared with laughter and walked out of the restaurant, tipping their ball caps to the crowd.

"You do know how to meet people, Billy, I'll give you that," said Max.

Billy waited for another call of "Roll" and raised his hand. This time, the waiter tossed it underhanded, and Billy squeezed it with both hands. The diners applauded this effort, and Billy beamed at his accomplishment.

"Uh, Billy, you might want to let that roll breathe a little."

Billy looked at Max, then down at his hands. He grasped the roll so tight, it had nearly returned to dough as it squeezed out between his fingers.

Chapter 14

Karl and Jimmy strolled through Bea and Al's front parlor the morning following their arrival. They were dressed casually; Karl had planned a walking tour of Logansport and felt an Armani suit amongst a crowd of bib overalls would draw attention.

"What time do you think the old lady serves breakfast, boss?" Jimmy asked.

Karl clicked his tongue in a bit of disgust. "How many restaurants do I own? Do you think I'm gonna even try to stomach whatever grits and pig knuckles Ma Kettle tries to serve us? Don't be..."

"Morning, boys," Bea called as she came into the parlor from the sitting room. "I hope you slept well, Mr. Jenkins. You, too, Mr. Hundley." She pushed apart two pocket doors that disappeared into the wall, revealing the dining room. At one corner of the large dinner table sat a man with a gray ponytail, reading the *Logansport Lookout*.

"Oh, everything was fine, Bea, just fine. We especially enjoyed the community bathroom at the end of the hall. How...rustic."

"Well, good!" she said. "Now, you two head into the dining room. Our other boarder, Dan, is in there and Al's getting the rest of the breakfast on the table. Go on, now!" She shooed them toward the dining room; Jimmy didn't need any coaxing, of course, considering he was in a perpetual state of hunger, but Karl protested.

"Oh, really, Bea, we ate a late dinner last night, and thought we'd just head into town..." Karl put his hand on Bea's shoulder. "Besides, I wouldn't want to put you to any extra trouble, dirty dishes and so forth."

"It's no trouble for this 'old lady,' Mr. Jenkins, it's part of the package. You know, bed AND breakfast."

Karl cleared his throat, a little embarrassed that he'd been overheard. "Yes, yes, but we're really in a hurry. Perhaps tomorrow." He turned to Jimmy, who had been drawn further into the dining room by the aroma of biscuits and sausage gravy. "Mr. Hundley…"

Karl headed for the front door. Jimmy leaned over to Bea as he passed her, and whispered "Save me some for later!" Bea nodded and winked at Jimmy.

As the front door closed, Al emerged from the kitchen carrying a plate of pancakes and a pitcher of syrup. "Where'd those guys go, Beatrice?"

"Oh, they've got business to see to in town. Too bad, they don't know what they're missing!"

Dan put down the paper, and stabbed the top four pancakes from the stack. "I don't know, Bea. That Jenkins fella seems a bit odd, doesn't he? I tried to be social last night after I got back from the station, but he didn't say two words to me. Acted kind of snotty, now that I think about it. Of course, he was brushing his teeth when I came in to shower, but…"

"They're paid up in advance, Dan. They can be as odd as they wanna be." Al skipped the pancakes, tore open a couple of biscuits and drowned them in gravy. "Right, Beatrice?"

Bea watched the two men disappear down Locust Street, headed toward downtown Logansport.

"Pig knuckles, huh?" she said under her breath.

* * *

Max and Billy had spent the night in St. Louis, with Max splurging on a room at the Adam's Mark Hotel. Their fifteenth-floor room faced the Mississippi River, and the famous Arch was right across the street. Looking out, Max could see the different riverboat casinos on both sides of the river; the city of East St. Louis, on the Illinois side, was attached to St. Louis by several bridges spanning the Mississippi.

They stopped in Springfield, Illinois, the next day when Max saw a sign for the old Route 66. But some legends are better left in one's memory; this section of Route 66 was just another road through town, and deadended at one point. Disappointed, he and Billy headed back up Interstate 55 towards Chicago.

By lunchtime, they were just west of Joliet, where I-55 and I-80 meet. They found a truck stop, as Billy wanted to grab a few local papers and Max needed to gas up the Lincoln. Billy disappeared into the diner while Max pumped the unleaded. When he finished, he pulled the Lincoln into a spot by the diner, locked it up and went in.

Billy was seated at a booth along the window, his head buried deep in a newspaper called *The Deaconville Democrat*. Max sat down across from Billy. "So, you think the rain'll hurt the rhubarb?" Billy didn't answer. Max scanned the front page of the paper. "Well, look at that. They put in a stop sign over by the courthouse. Guess we better stay out of Deaconville, huh, Billy? Sheriff Taylor and Deputy Fife must be writing tickets all day long over there."

"Hey, Max, check this out," Billy said, oblivious to his uncle's comments. As a waitress poured two cups of coffee, Billy read a letter to the editor about a church that was in danger of being closed.

"What about it, Billy? Churches close every day. New ones open every day. I don't see…"

"This is it, Max, I just know it. This is where I can help."

"How? What do you know about churches or fundraising?"

"But see, that's not the point, Max. We agreed that when I felt it was right, we'd stop. And Max, this feels right to me. Okay?"

"Okay, kid. So where is this church, anyway? And who wrote the letter?"

"It's St. Mary's Church in Logansport, Illinois. The letter was signed by someone named Maggi Kelly."

Max pulled the Illinois map out of his jacket pocket. "Logansport, C-9," he said. He followed the letter C down the grid of the map until it intersected with 9. Logansport was barely sixty miles east of the truck stop. "Well, the good news, Billy, is that we can be there in about an hour. The bad news is that if either of us blinks, we'll miss the town."

"C'mon, Max, let's go find this Maggi Kelly."

Chapter 15

"Well, hello, Maggi! What a pleasant surprise! Please, come in." Grace Wilson was just unlocking the front door to the Ben Franklin as Maggi walked up. "Ernie's home this morning, a little under the weather, so I've got the duty."

"Oh, I hope it's nothing serious, Grace," Maggi said.

"I don't think so, dear. You know, ever since he turned eighty he thinks he can complain about every little ache and pain. Really, men...but you didn't stop by to listen to my complaints, did you, Maggi?" Grace flipped on the fluorescent lights overhead.

"No, Grace, I just needed someone to talk to about St. Mary's. You and Mr. Wilson are the most senior parishioners and the most generous with your time and donations, and I just wanted you to know I'm not taking the Bishop's decision lightly."

"I know you're not, dear." She slowly climbed onto the stool behind the cash register, where she would spend most of the day. "In fact, I was just telling Ernie the other day how obvious it is that you love being the children's choir director. You can see it in your eyes and your smile, dear. And when those little angels sing, why, the same look is on their faces! It's just beautiful, Maggi, and it's what tells Ernie and me that St. Mary's is in good hands with young people like you."

"Thank you, Grace, you're right. I couldn't imagine what it would be like without my choir. Or St. Mary's, for that matter..."

"I know. It seems like those in power tend to forget the importance of history and of family. St. Mary's is our home away from home, and now they want to kick us out of our home. It's just not right,

Maggi." Grace looked out the large windowpane of the Ben Franklin. Maggi thought she could hear a tremble in Grace's voice that wasn't there before.

Grace looked back towards Maggi, and extended her hand. Maggi accepted it in both of hers, giving it a gentle squeeze. "Don't worry, Grace," she said. "Maybe what St. Mary's needs is a little divine intervention. Somehow, I don't think my great-grandfather Seamus would put up with this."

"He was a good man, dear. I guess it couldn't hurt to ask him if he's got any connections up there."

Maggi smiled. "I'll get right on it. Right now, I need to let you get to work, and I've got to get over to church." She walked over to the door and opened it; the tiny brass bells hanging just above it jingled as the top of the door knocked them sideways. "I'm working part-time with Father Bob, trying to organize all of the church records down in that basement, just in case…well, you know."

"All right, Maggi. Thanks for coming by."

"Bye-bye, Grace. Tell Ernie to feel better!" She waved through the window as she headed down the street. Lost in her thoughts, she barely noticed the aging Lincoln Continental as it pulled into a spot in front of the post office across the street.

* * *

"The post office, Max?" Billy looked up and down the street for a sign of life. No one, save for a man sweeping the sidewalk in front of an auto parts store a few doors down.

"Sure, kiddo. My guess is everybody knows everybody around here, and we can get this Maggi person's address from the clerk. Come on." They climbed out of the Lincoln and walked into the building.

The lobby of the post office was dark and quiet. A single overhead bulb hung behind the counter, barely illuminating the rows of routing baskets against the back wall. Max walked up to the counter, and tapped the silver bell.

A man in his fifties strolled out from a back room. "Keep your shirt on, I'm comin'. And quit ringing that dang bell." Without looking at Max or Billy, he pulled up a stool. "Now, then, what's wrong today...?" He paused, looking at the two men. "Oh, sorry, boys, I thought it was Mrs. Drangle. She comes in every week 'bout this time complainin' about the mail delivery. Woman hasn't had much more than bills and junk in ten years since her husband up and left her, and now she thinks we're holdin' her 'personal' mail. I tell her, you've gotta write letters to get letters, but does she listen? Nah." Max and Billy shook their heads, too.

"Course not. Goofy woman...you know what it is, don'tcha?"

"Uh, we really..." Max started.

"It's 'cause I wouldn't take her to the Sweet Corn Festival last year, that's what it is. So now she pesters me every week, sayin' all sorts of rotten things about the finest postal service in the U. S. of A. And now the Corn Fest is comin' up again next weekend, so I figure she'll be in here any minute, droppin' hints..."

"This is all very fascinating, my friend," Max interrupted, "but we just needed a little information, if possible."

"Oh, sure, sure. So whaddaya need, guys, stamps, envelopes, passports? We got it all!"

"We're looking for a girl named Maggi Kelly," said Billy. "We thought you might know where she lived."

"Yep, sure do." The man behind the counter leaned back on his stool, crossing his arms just under the U. S. Postal Service eagle patch on one side and a name tag on the other side announcing 'Hi, I'm Randall.' He then began gazing around the old lobby, whistling softly.

Max drummed his fingers on the counter. The whistling continued, punctuated by ticks from an ancient clock hanging over the door.

"Well, um...Randall, is it? Suppose you could share with us where she lives?"

"Not 'til I see the badges and warrants."

"The what?"

"What's she done? I always figured there was somethin' funny goin' on with her. Good cover, though…the kid's choir director. Yeah, right!"

"No, no, no. Nothing like that, Randall. We read a letter from her in a newspaper near here, and wanted to talk to her about it."

"Oh, you mean the St. Mary's letter? Well, why didn't you say so? Maggi lives over on Locust, number 314. Locust's a block west of Lincoln, that first street light down the way there." Randall pointed out the window past Max and Billy's Continental.

"Thanks, Randall, we appreciate it," said Billy, and the two turned away from the counter. As they did, a middle-aged woman came through the tall doors into the post office.

"That's it, Randall!" she shouted, as she brushed past Max and Billy. "The only thing in my mailbox yesterday was a PennySaver and a water bill. Give it up, mister, I mean it!"

"Uh, fellas," Randall called out, ignoring Mrs. Drangle, "you won't find Maggi at home right now, though. She's workin' part-time with Father Bob over to St. Mary's, as a matter of fact. You can see the bell tower just over those trees across the street and up the hill, there. She's either in the church basement or the rectory next door. Good luck!"

They waved back to Randall as Mrs. Drangle slammed her purse on the counter and crossed her arms. "Good luck to you, too!" Max called out, and then whispered to Billy, "I think Mrs. Drangle's looking for a special delivery, know what I mean?"

Billy, ever oblivious, said, "That costs extra, Max."

Chapter 16

"Father Bob?" Maggi poked her head through the screen door of the kitchen in the back of the rectory. She carried an old box of yellowing papers under one arm, and the musty smell told her it hadn't seen the light of day in many years. Wrinkling her nose, she set it down on the back porch. "Father Bob, what did you want to do with these old baptismal records?" No answer from inside the rectory.

She walked through the kitchen and down the breezeway toward Father Bob's office in the front of the building. "Father Bob?" she called again. Still no answer. She reached the pastor's office and saw the heavy oak door slightly open; a ray of sunlight from the window in the office split the darkness of the breezeway. Otherwise invisible dust particles darted through the sunlight beam, illuminating it enough to give one the impression it had form and shape and mass. Maggi thought maybe she could grab it like a lifeline, pulling her into Father Bob's office. She rapped her knuckle twice on the door.

"Father Bob?"

* * *

Robert Oliver was the youngest of six children given to Norman and Sally Oliver. The family had lived in the small bungalow on Chicago's southeast side since before Kenny, Robert's oldest brother, was born. The neighborhood around 110th and Avenue O was always diverse, at least as far as Robert knew. By his freshman year he was known as Bob, and he counted Poles, Italians, Mexicans, and African-Americans all as friends. It was the late 1970's, and Bob had always been the faithful child, as his mother put it. He attended mass at Queen of All Saints on a regular basis. After the requisite stint as an altar server, he volunteered in religious education classes. By eighth grade, he already had three times the number of service hours required by his parish for confirmation.

Norman Oliver had worked for nearly thirty years as a ladleman at the old Republic Steel plant a few blocks from their home until the mill was shut down when Bob was in grade school. After a few years, Bob seemed to feel that his dad had always been a house painter, the only job he could get after the mill. Because money was tight, Norman and Sally had to pull Bob out of Queen of All Saints' Catholic School after fourth grade. But Bob always sensed that his dad was doing all he could for his family, and accepted his assignment as a "public" graciously and without complaint. He found his mom crying in the backyard after his parents had broken the news to him, yet it was Bob who comforted her, telling her that maybe the public school was where God wanted him to go right now.

When he graduated from the seminary, his father had been gone for three years, taken by lung cancer from years of steel mill dust and soot. As a graduation present, his mother had taken their wedding bands and had them attached to the stem of a silver communion chalice. "Now go where God tells you, Robert," she said. After two years as an associate pastor in Minooka, Bob was named pastor of the storied but seemingly ancient St. Mary's in Logansport.

* * *

"Father Bob?" The aged door creaked open as Maggi stuck in her head into the office.

The large burgundy chair was turned toward the window. Father Bob sat with his elbows on the armrests, fingers crossed absent-mindedly, both index fingers extended together, pointing skyward. Dan Driscoll was introducing another oldie from the small radio on the credenza behind Father Bob's desk. He turned his head toward the office door.

"Oh, hi, Maggi. Done for the day?" He looked back out the window; the gardens of flowers planted by parishioners next to St. Mary's were losing their color this late in the summer. The tone of his voice made Father Bob sound distant; Maggi knew better. She sat down in the burgundy leather chair in the corner of his office. Father Bob continued to look outside.

"You know it's going to be all right," she said.

He sighed heavily and closed his eyes. "I was just thinking about the day I moved in, Maggi. Have you ever heard that story?"

"No, I don't think so."

Father Bob chuckled lightly. "What a day! I used to have this huge 1958 beige Plymouth, giant fins in the back, rust and duct tape holding everything together, you know the kind. Well, anyway, I had all of my worldly possessions in the trunk of that thing, books, clothes, everything. My mom, however, had given me a present–an old floral loveseat from her basement for my new home. All I could do was strap that thing over the trunk of the Plymouth. I hear I looked like the truck from the Beverly Hillbillies riding down Lincoln Avenue that day."

Maggi giggled. "Well, you had to get it here, didn't you?"

"Yeah. But you should have seen the look on Father Ed's face when I pulled into the driveway of the rectory. It was priceless. What a retirement gift he got that day!" He was standing now, looking out the window into the garden. "What a future for me…"

"You haven't given up, have you?"

"No, of course not, Maggi. But I'll tell you what, I've never felt so helpless in all my life. The Bishop seems to have his mind made up, and won't take any more IOUs. I know I've asked everyone to pray, but sometimes I think divine intervention only happens in those romantic comedies." He leaned in toward the window, craning to see towards the street.

"What is it, Father?" Maggi asked.

"I'm not sure, Maggi. One of those giant Lincoln Continentals just pulled in the driveway. What the…"

Maggi stood up and walked over next to Father Bob, peeking

around his shoulder.
"You know anyone from California?" he asked her.

Chapter 17

"And a good Tuesday to everyone out there, how's my adopted hometown of Logansport doing today? This, as always, is Dan Driscoll bringing you some of my favorite songs from yesterday along with all of today's news. Before we get back to the greatest songs of the greatest generation, I want everyone to be sure to offer a Logansport hello and welcome to Mr. Jenkins and Mr. Hundley, a couple of new boarders over at Bea and Al's with me. They're in town on business, they say, so let's make 'em feel at home. Maybe we can get 'em over to the Sweet Corn Festival this weekend, huh? Also, Grace Wilson tells me Ernie's feeling a little better, should be back to work at the Ben Franklin in the next day or two, and she wanted to pass on thanks for all of your good wishes and casseroles. In the meantime, here's a little Mel Torme..."

* * *

Karl and Jimmy stood outside of the Schwarz and Kelly Building, reading the dull bronze plaque, the same plaque Maggi Kelly touched for luck every time she walked by the place. Karl Schwarz harrumphed as he read the names of the 1959 town council that approved the memorial. "Bunch of rubes as I remember, Jimmy. My old man could have had this town eatin' out of his hand, they owed him so much. Not that he didn't profit from them, though. Nope, he built himself a tidy little fortune off of these John Deere jockeys, the old gasbag. From what I've been told, he invested some of it and gave the rest away to every Andy and Opie and Goober around here.

And I got a hundred bucks and a ticket to Chicago. Well, it's time to recoup what's rightfully mine, old Jimmy. What do you say?"

"I'd say I'm hungry, but you hate hearin' that." Jimmy took a step back out of instinct.

Karl just laughed. "You know what, Jimmy, I think it'd be news if you weren't hungry. C'mon, I wanna show you the rest of the town, and then we'll get somethin' to eat."

* * *

Max looked through the car's windshield at the old rectory. "Look at that architecture, Billy. This place is beautiful...reminds me of an old parish near where I grew up in New Jersey." He climbed out of the car and craned his neck up toward the bell tower.

Billy got out of the other side, and pushed the door shut. "Doesn't sound or look like anyone's here, Maxie."

The screen door of the rectory swung open, and Father Bob stepped onto the front porch. "It's always like that around here," he said. "Peaceful church, peaceful town. Hi, I'm Father Bob Oliver. Can I help you gentlemen?" He smiled and extended his hand.

Max and Billy came around the Lincoln to the front porch, each shaking Father Bob's hand. "How ya doin', Padre? I'm Max Duncan, and this is —"

"Billy Delaney!"

The three men looked back toward the rectory's screen door and the sound of the voice. Maggi stepped out, pointing at Billy.

"Billy Delaney," she repeated. "You were on *Where's Billy?* about ten years ago, then you kind of disappeared. I loved that show!" She was walking toward Billy now. "Whatever happened to you, Billy?"

Billy's cheeks were turning red, and he looked down at his shoes.

"My nephew's a little shy, ma'am, especially around such pretty young girls as you." Billy backhanded Max across the shoulder at this. *"Max!"* he said.

"But what's amazing here," Max continued, "is that we've been on the road for four days, met lots of people, and you're the first person to recognize Billy since we left California."

"You're kidding, right?" Maggi said. "Everyone around here loves *Where's Billy?* and they even show reruns on Saturday mornings on Channel 78 out of Springfield. I'd know you anywhere."

Billy looked up and extended his hand. "Thank you, um…"

"Maggi. Maggi Kelly." She gripped Billy's hand, holding it a second longer than usual. Billy looked into the most beautiful hazel eyes he'd ever seen.

"Meet pleased to you see," Billy stammered.

Max and Father Bob looked at each other, raising their eyebrows in that *Well, look what we have here* sort of way.

"We were hoping we'd find you, Maggi," said Max. "We've come because of your letter."

Maggi let go of Billy's hand, but not his gaze. "What letter?" she said, but then looked at Max and Father Bob. "Oh, the St. Mary's letter! But California? I only sent it to a few local newspapers. How did you–"

Max put his arm around Billy's shoulder. "Well, it's kind of a long story…"

Father Bob interrupted. "You know, we don't get many celebrities in Logansport. In fact, the last one I can remember was sportscaster John Madden's bus. Of course, John wasn't on it; they were just taking it over to Indiana for service. They do specialized work over in Indiana, I hear…"

"Wow, John Madden's bus," said Billy.

"Tell you what, gentlemen, it's almost lunchtime. I'd be honored if you would tell us your 'long story' over lunch. We've got a terrific family restaurant in town, the Purple Onion. I won't take no for an answer."

"Billy," Max said, "if there's one thing I learned in my life, when a priest wants to buy you lunch, it's a rare day indeed. Father Bob, lead the way."

* * *

Seated at the third booth from the window at the Purple Onion, Father Bob insisted Max and Billy try the Super Bird sandwich. The Super Bird was a hometown favorite, consisting of ham, turkey, and Swiss between two pieces of French toast covered in powdered sugar. On the side are a small bowl of raspberry sauce for dipping and a pile of seasoned fries. Billy finished his Super Bird in about five minutes as Max related the details of their brief journey. Maggi had a spinach salad, but most of it remained on her plate as she watched Billy vaporize his sandwich.

"Well, Billy, I must admit I admire your desire to do something worthwhile–not that being an actor doesn't have its pluses," said Father Bob. "But I'm not sure if there's much you can do for St. Mary's."

"Ah, that's where I come in, Father." Max wiped raspberry dip from his chin, crumpled the napkin and tossed it on his plate. "I've been thinkin' about this–if Billy is as popular around here as you've been saying, why couldn't we put something together where people pay five or ten bucks to meet him, have their picture taken, you know, the whole celebrity thing?"

Father Bob looked at Maggi. "Well, Max, with all due respect to you and Billy, we would need about 100,000 people to get in line in the next two weeks to meet our goal."

Maggi saw the dejection in Billy's eyes.

"Oh, yeah, you need about a half a mil, right?"

"Right. The Bishop's coming down this Sunday, and something tells me he's ready to pull the plug on St. Mary's. Our parishioners will have to drive all the way to St. Stanislaus in Kankakee or Blessed Savior in Belvedere, because building a new church here in Logansport is out of the question if the diocese can't even afford to repair this one."

"And I can't think of anything that would break more hearts," said Maggi. This time, Billy saw the dejection in her eyes.

Max held his coffee cup up as the waitress filled it for the third time. "Thanks, June," he said, reading her nametag. "Well, look, Father, maybe I need to noodle this a little longer. But something feels right, you know?" He tapped his chest. "You let us make a few phone calls, maybe we can get a little help going. In the meantime, I don't suppose there's a hotel near by, is there?"

Father Bob smiled. "Why, I just happen to know of the finest bed and breakfast within twenty miles. It's just a couple of blocks from here, great food, quiet, the whole nine yards."

"Sounds good to me. What do you think, Billy?"

"I, uh–what?" Billy looked away from Maggi toward his uncle.

"A room? What do you say?"

"Oh, thanks, that'd be great."

Father Bob smiled at Max. "Uh, c'mon Maggi, we need to get back to work. Let's show these boys how to get to Bea and Al's, and we'll finish up those baptismal records."

Maggi nodded, and the four slid out of the booth. Father Bob left a $20 on the table, waved at Eddie the cook and the people sitting at the counter–he knew almost everyone in town, Catholic or otherwise–and held the door for the others.

Father Bob didn't know the occupants of the fourth booth from the window at the Purple Onion, however. Two men. *Must be passing through*, he thought. He nodded at the younger man, who returned the recognition. An older gentleman with graying hair sat with his back to the booth Father Bob and the others had just left. He didn't look up.

Eddie wiped his hands on his apron and clicked on the old white radio next to the cash register.

"…And Sheriff Wilson said that whoever painted the fire hydrant should come down and talk to him, and he won't press charges. Honest. And just a reminder, the Sweet Corn Fest is this weekend at the county fairgrounds, so I hope to see you all out at my remote broadcast next to Mrs. Steenbauer's apple butter booth. Free tastes for the kids, you know. And now, how about a little Stormy Weather and the beautiful Lena Horne…"

Chapter 18

"Mrs. DeWerth, that had to be the best pot roast I've ever eaten."

"Well, I'm sure it's not as good as that tofu sushi stuff you boys get back home, Max. And for the last time, call me Bea or no dessert for you or Billy." Bea winked at Billy, who had already started his pie.

"Yeah, Beatrice, you really outdid yourself tonight. Well, I need a beer." Al scooted away from the dining room table. "Anybody else?"

Max and Billy shook their heads, and Dan Driscoll stood up from the table. "Much as I'd like to, I've got to get back to the station," he said. "Good night all, and Bea, I promise I'll fix that drain in the upstairs bath tomorrow."

"Thank you, Daniel, and be careful on your way back to the station." Bea looked at Max. "I just hate motorcycles."

Al returned from the kitchen, popped open his Stroh's and sat back down at the table. "So how long you boys think you'll be in town?"

"Don't know," Billy said. "We're going to try to do something to help St. Mary's and Father Bob, so I guess it will be at least until a week from Sunday."

"That is such a shame about the church, isn't it?" Bea started to gather a few of the dinner plates in one hand. "And that sweet Maggi Kelly's letter is what brought you out here. Could be another case of divine intervention, eh, Al?"

Al finished the last of the beer, and pulled another from his pocket. "What's the last case of divine intervention you ever heard about,

Beatrice?"

"When I found you, you little stud muffin!" Bea pinched Al's cheek, and headed for the kitchen. "And if you want to stay a stud muffin, no more beer tonight!" she called behind her.

"So, Al," Max said. "Are we the only boarders besides Dan?"

"Nah, we got a couple of guys down from Chicago for a few days. Say they're in Logansport on business. I guess they aren't too fond of home cooking, though, haven't had a meal here yet."

"No accounting for taste sometimes. Whaddaya say, Billy? I'm beat."

"Oh, you go ahead and turn in, Maxie. It's still kind of early, and since it's pretty warm out–"

"We call it Indian Summer out here, Billy," Al said.

"Well, I thought maybe I'd take a walk around Logansport, you know, see the sights."

"I'm not sure Logansport has any sights, Billy, but help yourself. Me, I'm sure I can find some game on some station." Al pulled another Stroh's from his other pocket and smiled at Max. "Good night, gentlemen."

Billy laughed. "Good night, 'stud muffin'."

* * *

The walk into downtown Logansport took Billy less than fifteen minutes. A late summer heat wave had left the air a little more humid than usual, and even with the sun setting, the temperature still hovered around 70 degrees, drawing beads of sweat to his forehead. Billy laughed at the thought that he couldn't remember the last time he had just gone for a walk; Max drove him everywhere, and besides, in L.A., people don't "walk" anywhere. Can't afford to be seen looking like one of those tourists, you know.

He turned on Washington, not really caring what street he was on. At the bottom of a hill, he came upon a gravel driveway. Looking up the drive through the trees, he saw a large white band shell surrounded by benches and folding chairs. It was draped all around in red bunting, and in the fading light he saw chairs and music stands under its roof.

Billy strolled up the drive to a small parking area. From there, a path led to the open area in front of the band shell. He picked out a bench a couple of rows back on one side, which allowed him to watch the sun setting through the trees behind it. *I didn't know these things really existed,* he thought. He put his feet up on the bench in front of him, leaned back and laced his fingers behind his neck.

"Mighty pretty, isn't she?"

The voice from behind him made him jump. He turned to see a small elderly gentleman in a short-sleeved white shirt, buttoned all the way up with a bow tie. He had his hands buried deep in the pockets of his baggy blue slacks that, held up by suspenders and a belt, seemed to come up somewhere above his navel.

"I'm sorry?"

"Oh, I'm sorry, son, didn't mean to give you a start. Mind if I join you?"

Billy looked around, wondering how this guy had snuck up on him so quickly. "Sure, I guess so," he said.

The man eased onto the bench a few feet from Billy, and exhaled deeply. "I've been out for my walk, and most nights I stop here for a visit. I was just saying how pretty she is."

"Yeah, it's a beautiful little band shell. Looks like they had a concert or something."

"Having," the man corrected. "Tomorrow night to kick off the Corn Festival. There's a jazz band that plays every year, local boys that sound like they're from New Orleans. You in town for the Fest?"

Billy thought about his answer for a minute. "Actually, I'm here for another reason, but we heard about the Fest and I guess we'll be there. Sounds interesting."

The old man laughed. "Yeah, it's interesting all right. A lot of fun, too, if you let it. So what does bring you to our little town?"

"Well, it may sound a little strange, but I think I'm here to help out at St. Mary's."

"You a carpenter?"

"Nah, nothing like that. I'm..." his voice trailed off.

"Plasterer?"

"No, I..."

"I know, an electrician. Those lights haven't worked right since the storm in '93."

Billy smiled at the man. "To tell you the truth, I'm not anything. I'm not really sure what I can do, but if Father Bob can find something for me, I'll do it."

"He's a good man, can see right inside people sometimes. He'll put you to work, all right."

A light breeze began to kick up, cooling their faces. Neither spoke for a few minutes. The sun was now a blaze of red between the trunks of the oaks. Back up the path, a group of children walked by singing.

The old man smiled at the sound. "Maggi must be having one more practice before Sunday."

Billy sat up a bit. "You know Maggi Kelly?"

"Sure, sure, everyone does. She's the sweetest girl this town's seen in years, save for my Grace. Maggi even wrote a letter to the newspapers tryin' to get help for St. Mary's. Say, that's who you are...you're that TV fella, whatsisname."

"I guess it's true what they say about word spreading in a small town. I'm Billy. Billy Delaney." He extended his hand.

"Oh sure, I remember you. You're that little rascal that couldn't stay out of trouble, right? Grace and I never watched that much television, what with the Ben Franklin and all, but we caught your show every now and then. My name's Ernie Wilson, Mr. Delaney." He took Billy's hand, and squeezed it as best as a man his age could.

"Please, it's Billy. Everyone's always called me that."

"Then Billy it is, so long as you call me Ernie. Yup, Grace heard down at the Purple Onion that you were in town, gonna help save our church now that you mention it. No offense, son, but what is it you think you can do?"

Billy turned almost as red as the setting sun. "My Uncle Max– he's traveling with me–thinks he has some connections in the national press. He says if he can get some reporters here, maybe we can get some donations. I don't know, it's worth a try. I just don't know if I'm enough of a draw to get much interest anymore."

"Sounds like you've kind of given up on yourself."

Billy just shrugged.

"Again, no offense, son, but we got enough defeatist attitude around here to fill a stadium. Look at you…you're young, got your whole future ahead of you. If you think you're done contributin' to society, you best think again. Look at me…I'm older'n dirt, and I run a successful business in town that fills a need. I've seen more down times than you could ever imagine, and every time I got knocked down a little, did I quit life?"

Billy looked up at Ernie. "No?"

"Of course I did," he laughed, "but it never lasted very long. I'd stand back up, dust off my knees and find a new direction. And what have I got to show for it? A pretty girl at home that fixes me dinner every night and still packs me a lunch for work every morning after almost seventy years of marriage. I've got the friendship of just about everyone in town. And up until the end of this month, I've had a house where I go every Sunday morning, kneel down, and say thanks for it all." Ernie folded his hands in his lap. "A little unsolicited advice, son. Maybe you need to stay away from that Hollywood, eh? I don't hear much good about that town, anyway. Now this," he waved his hand toward the band shell and Logansport in the distance, "this is a town."

"Thanks, Ernie. I'm going to see Maggi tomorrow. You're right, maybe I do have something to offer her." *Maybe she'll know what it is,* he thought.

Ernie stood up from the bench. "Well, I better head home, Grace'll think I'm sprawled out in a ditch somewhere. Anyway, welcome to Logansport, son." He took Billy's hand again. "And you know, when I said she was pretty, I was talkin' more about the sunset. Abe Lincoln once said that he could understand people lookin' up to Heaven and wondering if there was a God, but if we could look down from up there and see all of this, there'd be no doubt. Take care, son."

As Ernie slowly walked back down the path, Billy looked back through the pine trees around the back of the band shell. The sun was nearly gone now.

"You know, she's pretty, too," Ernie called from the end of the path.

"The band shell?"

"Maggi."

Chapter 19

The phone rang several times before it was answered.
"Yes?"
"Bishop Barnes, it's Father Oliver from St. Mary's in Logansport."
"Oh, yes, Robert, how are you this afternoon?"
"About as well as can be expected. I received your letter last week, and I understand you'd like to address the congregation this Sunday."
"That's correct, Robert. A 10:30 mass, I believe. You'll encourage everyone to attend that mass, I'm sure."
"That's our *only* Sunday mass, Bishop."
"Of course, of course. So what else can I help you with, Robert?"
The line was silent for a moment.
"Robert?"
"Well, I was just wondering if we could discuss your–the committee's decision. You see, I've been looking at some numbers, and I–"
"Robert, Robert, I've explained this before. It wouldn't be fair to you or your congregation for me to prematurely make any announcements. That's why I'm coming down to Logansport."
"I understand. I just wanted to let you know that we've had a bit of a difficult time raising $450,000 in pledges in the brief time you've allotted us. I was just wondering if you could see your way through to an extension of–"
"You should plan on Father Santos and me arriving sometime around 9:30, Robert. I trust you'll have lunch prepared?"
"Well, yes, but–"

"That's fine, then. We look forward to seeing you, Robert. I'm afraid I have to run. Please contact Father Santos if there is anything else I need to know. Take care, Robert."

The speakerphone button was pushed once to disconnect, preventing any response from being heard.

"He's a good priest, Bishop. We were a year apart at Mundelein, and he helped this young seminarian from Puerto Rico with his English on many evenings." Father Santos closed his writing pad and stood up from his chair.

"Miguel, I never said he was anything less than a competent pastor, but this is a financial arrangement we just can't let pass us by. That old building has been a drain on this diocese for more years than you've walked this earth. Karl Schwarz has promised us he'll maintain the integrity of the structure, hasn't he? How many parishes sit closed and empty around this country, Miguel? It's about time I started looking at this more with a businessman's eye and less with a sentimental one. That'll be all, Miguel."

Miguel stood there for a moment, taking in the Bishop's words. "Very well," he said. He turned and walked to the door of the office, pausing to look back as the Bishop's chair swung around to face the window.

"Oh, Miguel, one more thing."

"Yes?"

"I need a lunch reservation. Seafood would be fine."

Chapter 20

Max and Billy walked out onto the front porch after breakfast and found a white double-seat swing suspended by chains. Max sat down in the middle of it, his rather healthy backside taking most of each seat on either side. Billy pulled up a wicker chair next to the swing, just out of the sun. Al was arranging a hose and sprinkler on the front lawn, as Bea lectured him from a safe distance.

"You know, Billy, I could get used to this kind of life," Max sighed.

"We keep eating like this, one of us is going to get fat," Billy offered, laughing.

"I beg your pardon, nephew. I'm not fat, I'm short for my weight."

"Oh, is that it?" Billy picked up one of his Reeboks and gave the swing a push. It barely moved. "So what's the plan, Stan?"

"Well, while you were out for your stroll last night, I dug out my contact book. I'll spend the morning on the horn, you head on over to St. Mary's and find Maggi. I'm sure you two can find something to talk about."

Billy blushed. "You can stop that right now, Max. From everything I've heard, she's a very sweet girl with one thing on her mind right now, and it's saving St. Mary's. Okay?"

"Sure, sure, kiddo. Anything you say."

"Besides, if you'll recall, everyone keeps reminding me how I don't have a lot to offer. The same goes with girls, Max."

"Sure, sure, kiddo. Anything you say."

"You just said that!"

"Just pulling your chain, Billy. Go on down to St. Mary's, will ya?"

"All right, Maxie. Hey, this guy I met last night–Ernie something–said there's a concert in the park tonight to kick off the Sweet Corn Festival. Put it in your appointment book, okay?"

"You got it, buddy. See ya later."

Billy jumped from the front porch to the sidewalk, clearing three steps and jogged toward the street. He waved at Al, who had the garden hose wrapped around his left leg. Al saluted with the sprinkler, releasing eight streams of water across his pants, shirt, and face.

* * *

In the name of the Father, and of the Son, and of the Holy Spirit. Father Bob kissed the small gold crucifix hanging around his neck, a practice his mother had taught him. *Heavenly Father, I've come to you so many times over the past few years, I'll bet you're kind of tired of hearing from me.* The young priest rolled his eyes. *Sorry about that, I know better. Anyway–Father Bob here again. First of all, I'd like to ask your help in keeping everyone safe at the Sweet Corn Festival this weekend. Especially Mr. Dombrowski, who can't seem to remember to ride the Tilt-a-Whirl first and then eat. But most importantly, I'd like to ask one more time for your favor in helping keep St. Mary's open for the good people of Logansport. I've tried the Bishop, but you know how far that got me. Hey, believe me, I understand the gift of grace, though. I am willing to accept whatever may happen to St. Mary's, but that doesn't mean I won't fight to keep her.* Father Bob leaned back from the communion rail, and crossed himself. *In the name of the Father, and of the Son, and of the Holy Spirit.* "Amen," he finished out loud.

He stood, and from the back of the darkened church someone cleared their throat.

"Hello?" he called out.

A man stepped out from the last row of pews and walked back to the holy water reservoir on the wall next to the door. Father Bob couldn't make out his face; he never turned the lights on inside the worship center during the day, preferring to let God's sunlight pour through the massive stained glass windows. On this morning, the altar was brilliantly awash in colors. Mary stood to the right, her hands gently folded at her chin, her eyes fixed toward the middle pews as greens and yellows, blues and reds colored her white marble gown. Forty-four candles in red votive cups flickered all around her, lit by the faithful of Logansport praying for a reprieve.

"Hello?" Father Bob repeated, barely louder than a whisper. The word echoed around the worship center; the architects had designed St. Mary's arched ceilings so perfectly that one could distinguish between a slug and a quarter being dropped in a collection plate from the sacristy behind the altar.

"Sorry, Father, I didn't mean to disturb your prayers. I can come back another time."

"No, no, I was just finishing. I'm sorry, I can't see who's back there." The priest shaded his eyes, trying to get a better fix on the visitor.

"It's really not important, Father. I–I haven't been in a church for a long time. To pray like you were doing, I mean."

"Is there anything you'd like to talk about?"

"You mean, like a confession?"

"Well, most of us call it reconciliation nowadays, but sure, if that's–"

"Nah, I'll take a pass, Father. I think it's a little too late for a lifelong sinner like me. I hear it might be a little too late for St. Mary's, too."

Father Bob looked back at the altar, and over at St. Joseph's statue to the left. He was growing weary of the fight. "It would seem so," he replied.

Both men were silent for a moment.

"You know, Father, it really doesn't have to be this way."

"What do you mean?"

"Things ain't always the way they seem, know what I mean?"

"Well, sure, but what are you–"

"I really can't get into any details, but I like this place. There's somethin' about it, you know? The marble pillars, oak pews, everything just reminds me of my old church back home. Especially those windows, Father–they're beautiful. It would be a shame to see this all go away."

"I'm sorry, sir, I'm a little uncomfortable speaking with someone about this without proper introductions. I'm Father Bob Oliver, the pastor here at St. Mary's." He started toward the back of the church, but the man opened the center door.

"Uh, gotta run, Father, but right now, just keep in mind that things ain't always as they seem." He turned and went through the door before Father Bob was halfway down the center aisle, but not before reaching over and dabbing his fingers in holy water. The large oak door closed slowly, quietly.

Father Bob pulled the chamois rag from his back pocket and resumed wiping down the altar, going over the same area several times, wondering what in his world was not as it seemed.

Chapter 21

"Hi, Maggi."

Maggi was kneeling on the kitchen counter of the rectory, trying to reach a group of pans on top of the cabinet. Just as she looped a finger around the bottom saucepan, Billy's voice caused her to shriek as three copper-bottom pans caromed off of her shoulders on the way to the worn yellow vinyl floor. She turned in a completely futile attempt to at least catch a lid, and in doing so lost her balance.

Billy lunged forward. On another day, in another life, Billy might have tried to catch the falling pans. Today, Maggi fell backwards into his arms.

"Are you OK? I am so sorry, Maggi. I thought you heard me come in." She looked over her shoulder as Billy slowly backed her away from the counter, letting her feet fall to the floor.

She leaned forward away from him as she got her balance. "I-I'm fine, Billy," she said as she turned to face him. She could feel her cheeks turning red. "No, actually I didn't hear a thing." His own face turning bright red, Billy stepped back, kicking one of the pans across the floor and under the kitchen table.

"Not a great way to start, huh?" he said. He knelt down and picked up a couple of lids. Maggi couldn't help but laugh at the thought of this television star cleaning up her mess in the kitchen of an old rectory in a little town in the middle of nowhere.

Billy handed Maggi the lids and his red face gave way to a smile. "I seldom get that kind of reaction anymore, Maggi. Thanks."

"So, Mr. Delaney–"

"Please, Billy."

"All right, Billy. I guess you'd like to know what we're up against here at St. Mary's." She matched the pans with the lids and set them on the stove. "I'm making a little lunch for Father Bob right now. Let me get things settled here and I'd be happy to fill you in."

"Well, I did get a fair idea yesterday down at the Purple Onion. Father Bob's a pretty good guy, isn't he?"

"The best. But when he gets going about St. Mary's, I worry that he's got so many emotions, he loses sight of reality. Maybe you noticed yesterday that he's almost convinced St. Mary's is going to close, and I guess I can understand that. This is our home. And the diocese is trying to take it away from us."

Billy sat down at the kitchen table. "He really loves it here, I take it."

"We all do, but he does almost more than life itself." She pulled a bag of frozen vegetables from the refrigerator. "Tell you what, Billy. Why don't you go next door to the church—all the doors are always open, Father Bob insists on it—and take a look around. It's probably not much to look at in your eyes, but maybe you can gather your thoughts. I'll come and get you when lunch is ready."

"Sounds good, Maggi. Yeah, I figured the doors were open. Saw some guy coming out the front when I got here. Hey, listen, I think before I get to far involved in this, there's something you ought to–"

An old yellow wall phone at the end of the cabinets rang, and Maggi picked up the handset. "St. Mary's rectory," she said.

Billy waved to her, forgetting his thought, and walked back down the center hall of the rectory to the front screen door.

* * *

Billy walked back out the front door of the rectory and surveyed the front yard. A flagstone path led straight down to the sidewalk, where a worn bronze plaque with the words "Rectory of St. Mary" was embedded in a small brick pillar. On the inside of the pillar embedded in the mortar were rusted hinges, all that remained of some long discarded iron gate. Splaying skyward on both sides at the end of the path, wild orange daylilies formed a natural barrier between the front lawn and the sidewalk. The path itself was lined with the last remaining peonies of the season.

To the right of the front door, a small gravel path led to the side of the church less than fifty yards from the rectory. Billy stepped off the small red brick porch and walked towards St. Mary's. At the side of the rectory, he noticed a life-size statue of a woman with two curved benches in front of her. Several small bouquets of flowers sat at her feet, some faded, some fresh. Billy paused for a second. *Oh, yeah, St. Mary,* he thought.

The edge of the rectory lawn became the gravel side drive of the church. Billy stood on the edge of the grass and looked up at the massive bell tower.

"Sanctuary!" he said a little too loudly, then looked around to see if anyone had heard his Quasimodo impression. Only a cardinal's whistle from an elm tree came back as a critique; he hurried across the drive and up the four steps to the side door of the church.

Just inside the door, a set of stairs to the right went up five steps to a short landing, and then made a u-turn and continued back up over the entryway. This caused the ceiling to angle inward, stealing most of the headroom for anyone over four and a half feet tall. Billy ducked down and reached for the worn brass handle of the inner door. It turned easily; he pulled the door open and walked through.

Billy found himself on the right side of the church at about the middle pew. A quick glance told him there were approximately forty rows of pews on each side. Each pew appeared to be one single, long bench the width of the church with only a break in the center for the aisle. On the outside ends of the pews were hand-engraved words and numbers; Billy knew enough to recognize Bible passages, but had no idea of the text they represented.

Along the side walls of the church were round marble pillars each spaced a few feet apart. The white of the marble was offset by streaks of brown and gray; the same natural pattern and colors filled the large tiles affixed to the walls. Between each pillar at about eye level were what appeared to Billy to be small bronze figurines of a man in different positions; in some he held a cross, in others were more than one person. Beneath each figurine were sequential Roman numerals. Billy had no idea what these meant.

He looked left towards the back of the church. Along the wall towards the corner was what appeared to be a series of closets, each with a small light fixture over its door. He looked to the right, his eyes falling on the large wooden cross suspended by cables over the altar. The cross was easily fifteen feet tall and ten feet across; the timbers were square and thicker than railroad ties. At the center, the body of Jesus had been carved out of the wood so that he appeared to be inside of the cross; the day's sunlight illuminated a giant circle stained glass window behind the cross. The round window reminded him of those kaleidoscope toys with the bits of colored plastic in the end; the pattern at first look was random, but as a whole was soft, almost soothing to his eyes. From his vantage point, Billy could detect streams of colored light coming from spaces between the arms and legs and the wood of the beams, giving the cross the appearance of being part of the stained glass window. Billy took it all in; the silence of the great space only seemed to enhance its beauty.

His eyes saved the best for last, though. Billy stepped into a pew and walked towards the middle. He stopped and sat down, noting how the gentle curves in the bench fit him perfectly. When was the last time he had been in a church, he wondered?

He cupped his hands behind his head and looked toward the ceiling. From this position, his eyes caught the brilliance of a dozen different colors streaming from right to left in the air above his head. From the front to the back, the curves of the arches in the ceiling were ablaze in every color of the spectrum.

Billy's hands slowly separated as he followed the beams of light to their source. Beginning about two feet above each bronze figure and its Roman numeral were the most beautiful stained-glass windows he had ever seen. The late-morning sun on the east side of the building had cleared the roof of the rectory and the trees around it, and was now concentrated on the side of the church and its seven windows. Each window was four feet wide and stood fourteen feet tall. Seven other windows were on the west side of the church with a large square masterpiece above the doors in the rear of the church The detail within each window was magnificent. Groups of bearded men in brightly colored robes appeared in most scenes. Some knelt, some stood, and most often a single figure centered the glass as the others gazed at him reverently. Most scenes appeared to be in gardens or other outdoor settings, giving the artist the ability to showcase dozens of varieties and colors of flowers. The skies in the middle windows were not just blue, but every shade of blue with clouds from white to dark gray interspersed throughout. The windows on either end depicted skies of pinks and oranges and purples, completing a morning to night panorama across both walls of St. Mary's.

"My God," Billy whispered, "this is beautiful."

He still couldn't remember the last time he had been in a church of any kind, much less prayed. He'd always heard the jokes about Catholics and the constant up-and-down on their knees during church. His foot found the kneeler under the pew in front of him, and pulled it back into position on the floor. He thought about it for a second, and then slid from the pew onto the kneeler. He folded his hands in front of him and closed his eyes.

Dear God, my name's Billy Delaney, but then again, you probably knew that. This is it, isn't it? This is what I was supposed to find.

Billy Delaney opened his eyes and looked skyward.

"Thank you," he whispered.

Chapter 22

"Mr. Jenkins, you'll do nothing of the kind. You haven't taken a single meal with us since you got here, but tonight's a little special. Every year before the concert in the park, Al fires up the Weber for hot dogs for the neighborhood. You are going to the concert, aren't you?"

Bea had surprised Karl and Jimmy from the porch swing as they returned from their morning in town. Now she stood nose to nose with Karl, and she was getting a little irritated by their constant refusals for meals.

"Aren't you?"

"Actually, dear lady, I hadn't planned–"

"Well, now you've got plans. This town may seem a little sleepy to you folks, but we can really turn it on when we want to. You'll see. Now look, Al should have everything ready around five. Put on a pair of jeans, if you own any, and come on down. You too, Mr. Hundley."

"Looks like we have a dinner date, Mr. Hundley," Karl said, bowing his head ever so slightly to Bea.

"Sounds good to me, Mr. Jenkins."

"Very well, Beatrice, we'll see you in a couple of hours." Karl opened the screen door and walked into the parlor, letting the door shut on Jimmy.

"Sorry about him, Bea, he's just not the sociable type outside of work."

"Oh? And what is 'work,' Mr. Hundley?"

"He didn't mention it? Why, he owns one of the biggest chains of specialty rest–" Jimmy caught himself. *No one knows who we are or what we do until I say it's okay to tell them, got it?* Jimmy remembered the orders from the night they checked in.

"–uh, specialty rest stops. You know, those fancy places off the major toll roads. Very upscale, very cool, you know? Yep, specialty rest stops. That's my boss!"

Jimmy smiled, and hurried after his boss into the bed and breakfast.

Al had appeared from the side of the house carrying the charcoal grill. He was already wearing his apron, a long red one that said "King of the Grill" across the front. "What's up, sweet cakes?"

"Two more wieners for dinner, Al."

* * *

"Billy?"

He hadn't heard the side door open, nor did he realize Maggi was standing directly behind him as he knelt. He tried grabbing the back of the pew in front of him as he turned with a jump; his left knee came off the kneeler as his left foot slid under his right, causing him to fall face-first into the aisle at Maggi's feet.

"You know, seriously, we've got to start announcing ourselves a bit earlier," he said.

Maggi extended her hand and helped Billy up. He held her hand for a brief second longer than one would expect from a casual acquaintance. She looked down at his fingers, and he quickly let go.

"You O.K.?" she smiled, almost laughing.

"Yeah, thanks." He looked around the church. "I was just sitting here admiring this beautiful building."

"Then I have to say thanks again, Billy. My great-grandfather Seamus helped design and pay for it. I just love it here…" Her voice trailed off as she sat in the pew behind Billy's.

Billy eased past Maggi into the pew and sat down next to her. This was a little awkward for him; he felt he should offer some sort of comfort, but he couldn't recall a time when anyone had ever asked him to do so. Maggi's hands rested in her lap as she looked away from Billy. It was all he could do to reach over and give them a pat, and after he did, he looked away from her, too.

"My mom and dad were married here twenty-four years ago," she said. "They didn't have videotape back then, you know, so my mom's aunt took one of those black cassette tape recorders–I think it was a General Electric, you know, where the door pops up–anyway, she took the tape recorder and put it right up there on the kneeler in front of the communion rail. Well, they all thought they were state of the art, you know? Unfortunately, Aunt Ellen only used a sixty-minute cassette, so right in the middle of the priest's homily, the tape recorder shut off, so she had to tiptoe up to the communion rail and flip the tape over. Father was not amused."

"So do you ever pull out that tape and listen to it?"

"I didn't even know it existed until four summers ago. It was between my sophomore and junior year in high school, and I had just begun volunteering here at St. Mary's. I usually came home for lunch a couple of days a week. One day, I came home and my daddy's car was in the driveway. I went through the front door, and he was sitting by himself in the kitchen, listening to that tape."

"Why?"

Maggi didn't answer. Instead, she looked up towards the front of the church and the altar.

Billy looked in the same direction. "Oh. Oh, I'm so sorry, Maggi, I didn't know."

"It's okay, Billy, how could you have known? It was a simple stroke, a stupid little blood clot no bigger than a baby tooth. One minute, she's trying on dresses over at the Kohl's in Manteno, the next minute I'm the one shopping for a black dress in the same store."

She sniffled a little and brushed away some invisible lint from her jeans. "I do miss her, even though I've got Daddy to take care of and my work here at the church to keep me occupied. Sometimes, a person just needs their mom, you know?"

"Most people, I guess. My mom and dad ran off with almost every penny I made the first four years of my show. Nearly half a million bucks. Uncle Max took 'em to court, but the money had somehow vanished, so the judge ordered me into Max's custody. After the trial, they vanished, and we never heard from them again. That was seven years ago, Maggi. I used to miss her. I thought she'd miss me, too."

"I'm sorry too, Billy."

They both sat silently for a moment. Maggi then took Billy's hand.

"Funny, isn't it?" she said. "Here, we've got a Catholic church that's short about half a million bucks, and you had that much, but it was stolen from you. Now, they want to steal our church from us, all our memories, and all our futures."

"And me out looking for my future, right?"

"Yeah, something like that. But I don't have to tell you, Billy, that a good Christian is willing to accept whatever happens in a tough situation, right?"

"Uh, sure. You know that reminds me. I may not be qualified...um, how do I say this..."

"OHMIGOD!" Maggi shouted as she grabbed Billy's arm.

"What?"

"I left the vegetables boiling on the stove! C'mon!"

The two stood up and bolted out the side door of the church with Billy firmly smashing his forehead on the low ceiling beneath the choir loft stairs.

Chapter 23

"That's about it for me, folks. This is Dan Driscoll, and I've got to head over to Bea's for the annual hot dog roast. The concert starts in a little less than two hours at the band shell, so I'll sign off for now and pick it back up with my remote at seven o'clock. You all be sure to stop over and say hey, will ya? In the meantime, I'll leave you with a little preview of tonight's festivities. Here's Miles Davis and a selection of his greatest jazz hits..."

* * *

Twice a year, Al barbecued on the front lawn of the bed and breakfast. The first occasion was the Fourth of July, when their corner yard was a perfect viewing location for the parade. Most everyone on the block congregated in the yard and the tree lawn along with coolers and folding chairs, and Al provided hot dogs at no charge.

The parades were typical small town. Antique cars carried local politicians and business owners, and a restored olive drab Jeep carried all four members of the VFW. Local farmers painted their old Massey Ferguson and FarmAll tractors and pulled wagons filled with Cub Scouts and 4-H kids right past Bea and Al's. And there was also the tradition of The Pyramid. At certain points in the parade, a tractor would almost always break down, causing a large gap in the procession. When the gap would reach the corner of the bed and breakfast, any man who had accepted a free hot dog had to run out into the street and form a human pyramid. Al DeWerth was always the center of the bottom row along with the other huskies. The point of the pyramid was usually someone's girlfriend or fiancée. They would hold the pyramid, as the crowd on both sides of the street would count off "One, two, three..." in unison as knees trembled and shoulders waved back and forth. The record was twelve.

The other occasion for Al's front yard feast was the Concert in the Park before the Sweet Corn Festival. The Sweet Corn Festival was the area's traditional end of summer celebration. Town elders remember the first festival being held sometime in the late 1920's, not too long after St. Mary's first open her doors. It had been held off and on over the years depending on the town's coffers, and a year without a festival almost always meant a new tax referendum the following spring.

The location itself had moved over the years as well. During the early years right up through the end of World War II, it was held right in the center of town. With very little traffic in those days, businesses would throw open their doors for the curious from other parts of the county who came by bus to ride the rides and play the carnival games. In effect, the local shops became part of the Sweet Corn Festival.

When America mired itself in another war, this time in Korea, the festival went dormant until 1954. That year, Gerhard Schwarz and Seamus Kelly offered the empty fields behind their grain elevator, and the town graciously accepted. As the grain elevator was less than one-half mile from town on Route 47, someone suggested that the town's brass band, which had performed every year during the fest, should lead a parade out of town to the new location at the beginning of the weekend.

This tradition carried on until 1968, when a new generation seemed to turn its back on such homespun entertainment. The membership of the brass band had dwindled through retirements or other interests, and eventually it was dissolved. The people of Logansport seemed to spend a few years simply going through the motions of life. The downtown area began to show its age, and little was done to resuscitate its seemingly terminal disease.

Then in 1974 the high school hired a new band director, Luke

Donahue. Within five years, the Logansport Lions Marching Band had twice taken first place honors in the Class A division at the state competitions in Champaign. Its Wind Symphony regularly was recognized as one of the finest of all small-sized schools anywhere in the state.

But Luke "the Don" Donahue, despite being a young man at the time, was an aficionado of jazz (and an expert on The Godfather movie, giving him his nickname). Not the "smooth jazz" of the present but the New Orleans-style of the past. A piano, saxophones, trombones, drums, a standup bass and maybe a clarinet would complete his ensemble, and he insisted on the best.

Only after he was satisfied that he had a jazz band worth listening to did he enter them in a regional jazzfest. The music that poured forth that afternoon stunned the audience. With its tight, crisp horns and Buddy Rich-inspired drum solos, they walked away with top honors. That spring of 1982, a new sign welcomed visitors to Logansport, "Home of Illinois' Finest Brass Band."

Luke tried to explain to the mayor the difference between a jazz band and a brass band, but the sign had already been painted, and old Mr. Kettleman would charge a fortune to repaint it. So brass band it was, and remains to this day.

Two years later, the Caterpillar plant over in Grundy County donated $10,000 towards a park improvement program. Nostalgia fueled a proposal for a band shell, and fearing they would waste the money if they didn't spend it, the city council contracted for one the day after it was proposed.

As the Mi-Jack crane slowly lowered the roof onto the band shell, it was former city councilman Stuart Philkins (the band shell proponent) who casually commented that it would be even better if Logansport had a band to play in their new band shell. After an emergency session, the city council settled on two items. First, to never again entertain proposals from Stuart Philkins, and second, to ask Luke Donahue if his jazz band would be available for a grand opening concert.

And so, the Concert in the Park was born. Over the years, it was scheduled closer to the Sweet Corn Festival, eventually settling on the Friday night before. Former jazz band members who had graduated and still lived in the area sat in on the concerts, relishing in the opportunity to play for "the Don" one more time. Eventually, the band shell became a bit crowded, and Luke had to limit membership to twenty players.

In the twenty years since, Bea and Al purchased the bed and breakfast just two blocks from the park. And every year, as the people of Logansport would take an early evening walk on a late summer's Friday to hear some incredible music, most everyone would stop in to say hi to Al, munch a hot dog and drink a beer, and complain about the Cubs and their annual swan dive. This year would be no exception.

Chapter 24

After lunch, Billy and Maggi spent the afternoon talking about ways that Billy could draw some attention to St. Mary's. Billy explained that his Uncle Max was an old hand at publicity, and it shouldn't be a problem. Even with a few days before the Bishop's arrival, Billy promised that they could get something on one of the cable shows fairly quick. "If they could show the plight of the church on a national level," he said, "maybe the Bishop might give them a reprieve."

Maggi could feel a sense of hope for the first time. As Billy stood from the kitchen table at the rectory, she threw her arms around his neck, tears building in her eyes.

"Oh, Billy, if this could happen, I wouldn't know how to repay you," she almost sobbed.

Billy wasn't quite sure how to react. Slowly he put his arms around her and patted her back.

"Hey, hey...come on, now," he whispered. "We can do this."

Embarrassed, she stepped back and wiped her eyes.

"Tell you what," he said. "Come on over to Bea and Al's this afternoon before the concert. We'll see what old Maxie has come up with, and take it from there. I hear Al grills a mean hot dog."

"All...all right. I've got to stop home and see if my dad wants to go to the concert, though. This is the first year he's been off work for it in a long time."

"Well, bring him, too. I'd like to meet him, Maggi."

* * *

Billy bounced down the street on his way back to Bea and Al's. As the occasional car would pass him, its driver would lift one hand in a "How ya doin'" motion. Billy thought it was great that so many people recognized him; little did he realize that the gesture was another part of small-town American courtesy. Everyone waved at everyone.

A dozen lawn chairs in a dozen different styles dotted the front yard of the bed and breakfast. It was four o'clock, another hour until the cookout, and no one was in sight, save for Max.

He was sitting on the front porch swing, his eyes closed. The only noise in the air was a chirping whistle in the trees behind and around the old home. The whistle started out in low, soft pulsating tones, gradually growing louder until it reached a crescendo and then abruptly stopped for a few seconds before starting again.

The grill and assorted chairs sat at the ready near the bed and breakfast sign on the lawn, a bag of Kingston charcoal briquettes and a can of lighter fluid nearby. The Lighting of the Grill Ceremony had almost become as big as the concert itself. Al's eyebrows always grew back, though.

"Hey, kiddo," Max waved to Billy.

"Hiya, Maxie–" Billy started, but Max put his finger to his lips.

"Shhh." He then waved Billy toward him and pointed at the empty seat on the porch swing. Billy took the steps in one jump, and plopped down next to Max.

"What's up, Max?"

Max again put his finger to his lips, but didn't say anything. He pushed off with his foot, and the swing gently rocked them. The afternoon sun had settled behind the house; the porch and most of the front yard were in shadows.

"You hear that, Billy? The sound in the trees?"

"Yeah. Gets awful loud, don't it?"

"D'you know what it is?"

Billy looked around a post on the porch toward a large oak tree on the side lawn. "I can't see anything up there, Max," he said.

"No, and you probably wouldn't, either, unless you climbed up there."

"What's making the noise?"

"Well, it's kind of a neat story. Dan Driscoll, the radio guy that lives here, was just tellin' me they're called cicadas. Here I thought I was gettin' a buzz in my ears, but it's nothing but a bunch of bugs in the trees."

"What's so neat about a bunch of bugs?"

"The thing is, these bugs only come out of the ground every seventeen years."

"Get out of town..."

"No, seriously. Millions of 'em. For the last seventeen years, these noisy little things have been living underground, munching on tree roots. Then, according to Dan, some sort of biological clock goes off; they all come up out of the ground at the same time, climb up into the trees and start that chirping. It sounds like one long continuous noise, but actually, it's millions of cicadas all singing to each other. They live in the trees for thirty to forty days, then head back down to lay their eggs and die. Seventeen years later, another group comes along and does it all over again. Unbelievable that we show up now to hear this, isn't it?"

"Nothing like this in California, huh, Max..."

The uncle and nephew swayed in the porch swing, taking in the free cicada concert.

"Billy..."

"Nobody's coming here, are they, Max," Billy said in almost a whisper.

"I'm sorry, kiddo. I must've made thirty calls today. No one seems to care about a church closing in some little–"

"They don't care about some has-been kid actor. You can say it."

"Aw, now, they didn't say that."

"They didn't have to. I'm not that stupid, Max." Billy stood up, walked across the porch and leaned on the railing. "I can deal with it," he said finally. "But what am I going to tell Maggi. Here I spent the afternoon getting her hopes up that national reporters might want to tell St. Mary's story. How big an ego could I have had?"

"Sit down here, Billy." Max patted the seat next to him on the swing.

After a moment, Billy returned to the swing.

"Have you already forgotten Caroline's advice? Whenever you do something for someone, do it in such a way that no one knows you're doing it. That's your reward, Billy. What did you think, that a convoy of TV trucks would show up, your face would be all over the country, and suddenly everyone would want to help St. Mary's?"

"No, but—"

"Somethin' tells me He don't work that way, either," Max said, pointing skyward. "You know, it's a funny thing. Most people spend their lives chasing things. The next paycheck, the bigger car, the better home in a nicer neighborhood, the perfect mate. They're chasing dreams, Billy. Yet it seems to me that all along, someone's right behind them, making them an offer they can't refuse, you know?"

"I'm not sure what you mean."

"It's like this." Max shifted in the swing to face Billy. "People chase dreams, it's true. But dreams come from in here." He tapped a finger on Billy's temple. "Not out there."

Over their silence, the cicada chorus began again.

Chapter 25

"Okay, who's ready here?" Al reached into the Weber and skewered a hot dog with a long fork, holding it high over his head.

"Sounds good, Al. Set me up."

Al turned to his left. "Patrick Kelly! Hey, great to see you, big guy. How you doin'?"

"Well, aside from two crummy part-time jobs, no health insurance and a bad back, I'd say I'm doin' great."

Al put his arm around Patrick's shoulder.

"You know, Patrick, my mother gave me a few words of advice on her deathbed for situations like this that I've never forgotten."

"What was that, Al?"

"She said, 'I think this calls for a beer.' BEATRICE!"

It was about forty-five minutes before the jazz concert, and the front yard of the bed and breakfast was crowded. Bea came through the screen door onto the porch, carrying two packages of buns and a stack of red plastic beer cups. She came down to the bottom step just as Al was yelling for her.

"WHAT!?" she screamed back. Unfortunately, she was standing directly behind Randall, the counterman at the post office. Randall jumped six inches, and his paper plate, holding a fresh scoop of potato salad, flew upwards over their heads. The creamy yellow ball separated from the plate, continuing on its path. With a decidedly loud bam it found the middle bedroom window on the second floor, where it stuck.

"Aw, Jesus, Mary and Joseph, Bea, I'm sorry," Randall said. They looked up at the window, where the ball of potato salad slowly slid down the windowpane, leaving behind a yellow trail.

Bea sighed. "That's okay, Randall, I can see I used too much mustard."

Ernie and Grace Wilson were now standing next to them, also looking up at the window.

"Nice shot, Randall. But the roof would have been really impressive." Ernie gave Randall a little nudge with his elbow. "Maybe next time, eh, killer?"

"Ernie, leave Randall alone," Grace said, grabbing her husband's elbow. "Come on, let's get you a hot dog." Ernie just laughed, and the two walked down the front lawn to the grill with Bea close behind.

Al waved his fork. "Hi, Wilsons!"

"Al, you almost made me give poor Randall a heart attack back there. What do you want now?" Bea set the buns down on the plastic table next to the grill.

"Look who's here, hon–Patrick Kelly! I thought you'd want to pour his first beer." Al slapped Patrick on the back.

"Well, Patrick–we've missed you at our Sunday afternoon dinners ever since…oh, I'm so sorry." Bea looked down, nervously removing the twist-tie from one of the bun packages. "You're not here even two minutes, and I'm talking about Virginia."

Patrick gave Bea a hug. "Hey, that's okay. I think about her all the time. Nice thing to do, I've decided. Anyway, Maggi decided she needed to take care of me, I guess, so she makes me dinner every Sunday. Just between you and me, Bea, I miss your dinners, too."

"I guess I just miss her too, Patrick, and seeing you here after so much time…" Bea's voice trailed off; Patrick squeezed her a little tighter.

"Hey, now," he said. "I think this calls for a beer. Al's mom said so."

* * *

A few minutes earlier on the second floor of the bed and breakfast, Karl Schwarz stood before a full-length mirror in his room, adjusting the crisp collar of his shirt. He had simply removed his suit jacket and necktie, and had replaced them with a gray Italian sweater tied loosely over his shoulders. *I may have to mingle with the rubes, but I don't have to look like one,* he thought.

Jimmy Dozan rapped lightly on Karl's open door. "Ready, boss?" Jimmy, however, had decided to try and blend in with the crowd. He sported his old Chicago Bears jersey, faded jeans and a pair of grass-stained Reeboks.

"You look like you like it here," Karl said, pulling out a pocket comb and running it straight back through his hair.

Jimmy plopped down in the easy chair next to the small desk by the window. "Well, I been thinkin', boss. Who you gonna get to run this restaurant down here? With all your other interests, I think I could handle it."

"Please, spare me your 'thinking', Jimmy." He replaced the comb in his pocket and looked at Jimmy's reflection in the mirror. "You just let me handle things, and do what I tell you. Have I ever let you down?"

"I know, boss, I know. It's just…well…"

"Well what?" Karl turned to face Jimmy.

"Well, you're right, I kinda do like it here."

"See? That's why I couldn't let you be in charge of anything. You 'kinda' like it here. Either you do or you don't–there's no room in this business for 'kinda' anything. Excuse me, Mr. Restaurant Manager, are your steaks good today? Well, kinda," Karl said mockingly.

Jimmy looked down at the floor, not saying anything.

Karl turned and walked over to him. He stood next to the window and towered over Jimmy.

"One must know one's place in life, Jimmy. Me, I'm a self-made success story. Nobody ever gave me anything; I had to do this all by myself. You, on the other hand, are a muscle-bound gopher who has needed every break you've ever gotten. If it weren't for me, you'd be bussing tables for minimum wage somewhere. That's the difference. When I needed something, I went out and got it. You have the nerve to ask for yet another break. If you're ever going to make it in this life, Jimmy, you're just going to have to make your own break, not ask for it!" By now, Karl's voice had gotten very loud, and the louder it grew, the tighter Jimmy closed his eyes.

Karl turned toward the window.

"Besides, who says I'm going to–"

At precisely that second, something smacked the window right at Karl's eye level. He flew backwards, landing on his rear end. Jimmy jumped out of the chair, stepping back as well.

"What the–" Karl yelled. He put his hand on the floor, struggling to stand up. Instead, his palm caught the back of his sweater, choking him and pulling him back down.

Jimmy walked over to the window.

"I'm not sure, boss, but I think it's…"

"It's WHAT!?"

"Um, potato salad."

Chapter 26

Max and Billy stood off to one side of the yard, out of the way of the plume of constant smoke from Al's grill.
The front lawn was now filled with people. In the distance, above the conversations, you could hear the jazz band warming up for the evening's concert. Max patted Billy on the shoulder.
"Hear that, kiddo? Sounds like they're getting ready for us. Now look, I won't say anything to that girl…"
"Maggi."
"Yeah, Maggi. And don't you say anything, either, all right? I'm not licked yet."
"All right," Billy said, but Max could hear the dejection in his voice.
"Billy!" Max and Billy turned, and saw Maggi coming through the gate. She waved at them, and then a few people in the crowd. She stopped on the sidewalk, scanning the yard, and then recognized someone near the house. She waved frantically in that direction, and a man came over to her. The two of them then turned and walked over to Max and Billy.
"Hi, Billy!" Maggi said excitedly, and then threw her arms around him. "I want you to meet someone very special to me. Billy Delaney, this is my dad–Patrick Kelly."
Billy extended his hand. "It's an honor to meet you, sir. Maggi only talks about you slightly more than St. Mary's."
Patrick reached out and shook Billy's hand. Billy could feel the calluses within the strong grip. Likewise, Patrick could feel the softness of a hand that had probably never held a hammer or a broom.

"That's funny, son, she does nothing but talk about you at home. The pleasure's all mine. I hear you used to be on TV or something."

"Daddy, you watched Billy's show with me every week. Stop it."

Patrick winked at Billy.

Max stuck out his hand, as well. "Hello, Patrick. I'm Max, Billy's sherpa."

Patrick shook Max's hand. "So, Billy even has 'people', eh? Pleased to meet you, Max."

"Yeah, in fact, I'm all of his people. Even his uncle."

Patrick smiled at Max. He knew right away that the two of them would get along.

"So, Billy," Patrick said, "my little girl tells me you've got a plan to help save St. Mary's. Are you gonna spring it on us at the last minute, or can you give us a hint?"

"Well, I..."

Max jumped between the two. "You know, Patrick, it's a work in progress. As soon as we have some definite plan of action, we'll fill you in. Say, where'd you get that beer?"

"Oh, right over th–"

Max grabbed Patrick's arm. "Come on, I'll buy you another as long as they're free."

Maggi and Billy stood alone now near an old willow tree in the corner of the yard.

"Oh, Billy, I'm so excited. I stayed at church and talked to Father Bob after you left. That's why I'm late. He was smiling from ear to ear when I left. Have I told you how excited I am?" She closed her eyes, clasped her hands under her chin.

"Thank you," she whispered.

"Say, listen," Billy stammered. "I'm starved, Maggi. How about one of Al's famous hot dogs?"

"I'd love it," she said. "We've only got a little time before the concert starts. Most of the kids from my choir will be there, and I want you to meet them."

Billy offered his arm, and they walked together over to the grill.

* * *

"Would you look at that, Al. They do know how to come out of their hole."

Karl and Jimmy stepped through the screen door and on to the front porch. Karl quickly removed a pair of mirrored sunglasses from his shirt pocket and put them on. He surveyed the crowd. *How in the world was he going to make his way through this human cornfield without actually talking to anyone*, he thought.

"Well, if it isn't our out-of-town guests, Al. Give 'em a dog."

Somehow, Bea and Al had come up on the side steps of the porch behind them. Jimmy smiled broadly; Karl remained stone-faced.

"Sure, sure, boys, here ya go." Al held out a hot dog in each hand, Bea a cup of beer.

"Oh, really, Mrs. DeWerth, we couldn't–" Karl started.

"Hope you've got seconds!" Jimmy said, taking the dog and beer.

"–possibly eat another bite," Karl finished, almost as quickly as Jimmy finished his hot dog.

"Don't be silly, Mr. Jenkins," Bea said, forcing the other beer into his hands. "There'll be no dinner here tonight, hot dogs is it. C'mon, eat up." She elbowed Al, who put the dog into his hand.

"Thank you so much, Mr. De–"

"Al."

"Ah, yes. Al. And thank you, Mr. Hundley," Karl said, glaring at Jimmy.

"Well, I'll tell you, boys, I'm sure glad to see you've decided to join us for the concert. Some of the prettiest jazz music on a cool autumn evening you'll ever hear." Bea squeezed in between Karl and Jimmy, and took each of them by the elbow. "Why don't you step down into the yard, and I'll introduce you to a few of our friends."

"How could we ever say no, Bea?" Karl said, a little too animated.

"You can't. Not to me. Come on."

Bea walked the two men around the yard, introducing them to almost everyone there. Betty Benjamin, of Betty's Sunflower Shoppe and Bea's best friend, told the two they should come over for a swim some evening. Dee Hensley and her daughter Laura operated a quilting store over on Locust Avenue, and wondered if Karl and Jimmy needed escorts to the concert.

"Gentlemen, I'd like you to meet two of our little town's greatest treasures. Grace, Ernie?"

Grace and Ernie Wilson turned toward them, and for a moment, Karl felt a little uneasy but didn't know why.

"This is Grace Wilson and her husband Ernie," Bea continued. "They own the Ben Franklin on Main Street."

Karl shook Ernie's hand, and taking Grace's hand, bent slightly at the waist and kissed it. "Mrs. Wilson, I'm charmed," he said.

"Oh, my, I don't think anyone's kissed my hand since–well, I don't think anyone's ever kissed my hand. How about that, Ernie?"

Ernie rolled his eyes. "Don't mind her, mister, she gets excited when they put extra napkins in the bag at the drive-through, know what I mean?"

"Yes, I'm sure that makes for an extra special evening for you two, eh?"

"I can see I'd better keep an eye on you, Mr.–"

"Jenkins. And this is my associate, Mr. Hundley. We're in rest stops."

"Um, excuse me?"

"Rest stops. You know, those little roadside conveniences on the interstate…"

Ernie looked at Grace. "I know what they are, Mr. Jenkins. What do you mean you're 'in them'?"

"Oh, I apologize, Ern. I mean we design and build them."

"Yes, of course you do, Jenk."

Karl looked at Jimmy. "Well, if Beatrice here has no objections, I think we should be heading on down to the park. Jimmy?" Karl motioned toward the sidewalk.

"It was certainly a pleasure meeting everyone, Mrs. DeWerth, especially the Wilsons here," Jimmy said. He gave a little wave and tottered off behind Karl, who had already headed toward the street.

"Interesting guests you've got there, Bea," Ernie said.

"I know what you mean, Ernie. They barely come out of their rooms, and when they do, they're gone for hours and never join us for dinner. Pretty rude, I'd say."

"Then there's that name thing."

"What name thing?"

"Oh, come on, you didn't buy that Jenkins and Hundley bit, did you?"

"I don't—"

Ernie harrumphed. "I forgot, you're from Cleveland. Fergie Jenkins and Randy Hundley were a pitcher-catcher duo for the Cubs in the 1960's. In fact, Jenkins made the Hall of Fame. No, that's too much of a coincidence."

"So what do you think, Ernie?" Al said.

"Beats me, Al. But there's something about that 'Jenkins' fella...he kind of gave me the creeps when he shook my hand. I wish I could figure out what it is."

Grace gave a tug on the bill of Ernie's ball cap. "Come on, James Bond. We've got a concert to get to, and then it's right to bed with you. You're still not one hundred percent, you know." With that, the two lovers and best friends slowly walked down the sidewalk, joining Billy, Maggi and the rest of the crowd already on their way.

Chapter 27

"Good evening, Logansport!" Dan Driscoll pulled the microphone from its stand and held it out to the audience around the band shell.

"Hi, Dan!" everyone shouted in unison. A group of little kids chased each other around the park, laughing and enjoying their freedom from their parents for the time being. The crowd cheered as Dan waved his hand upward, coaxing them on.

"It gives me great pleasure to introduce one of the best band directors this country's ever had–Mr. Luke "The Don" Donahue and his Logansport Jazz Band!"

The crowd erupted again, as Dan put the mike back in the stand and welcomed Luke to the stage.

"Thanks, Dan. Thank you, everybody," Luke said as the horn section behind him softly warmed up. Joe Shake, a tenor sax player who had graduated from the University of Illinois at Champaign, was making faces at a host of high school girls down in the front row.

"As it has been our tradition for the past, oh, I don't know how many years," Luke continued, "it gives me great pleasure to kick off the Sweet Corn Festival with Illinois' finest jazz ensemble!" He made a sweeping motion with his hands as the entire band stood and bowed.

"We'd like to begin this evening's concert with a perennial favorite…" An 'ooh' went through the crowd, followed by soft applause. Everyone seemed to know the opening song. Everyone, of course, but Billy and Max.

Billy leaned in to Maggi. "What's the song?" he said.

She put her hand on his. "It's wonderful, Billy. It's called–"

"Sweetheart of Mine," Max said from the other side of Billy as the first few bars of the song swept out over the crowd.

Maggi and Billy looked at each other, then at Max.

"Jelly Roll Morton. Recorded in Chicago, April of 1926, I believe."

Both Maggi and Billy's mouths dropped open in mock surprise.

"Whaaa?" they said in unison.

"What, you think I haven't had a life before you, kiddo? I've got a few things up in this noggin besides loose change." He smiled and closed his eyes, letting a drum solo take him back to a place Billy didn't know existed.

Luke Donahue's jazz band played for nearly an hour straight, with only slight pauses to introduce a song and its history. Billy heard many composers' names for the first time, Max for the thousandth. Names like Bix Beiderbecke, Charles "Cow Cow" Davenport, and Bubber Miley.

After a particularly rousing version of Fats Waller's "I've Got A Feelin' I'm Fallin'," Luke announced a fifteen-minute break so the band could catch their breath. Not a soul had left the park; Dan Driscoll was in his glory, and soon he and Max were discussing the lost greatness of 1920's Chicago jazz.

Billy and Maggi walked back to a row of folding tables, where the ladies of the Red Hat Society had set up pitchers of iced tea. Billy poured her a cup, and grabbed a sugar cookie from a paper plate.

"So what do you think?" Maggi said.

"I've never had a better sugar cookie."

"No, you goof. The band, the music. What do you think?"

"Oh. It's unbelievable, Maggi." Billy looked away, and didn't say anything else.

The silence between the two was nearly as loud as any piece from Luke's band. Maggi waited for him to say something else; when it became obvious that he wasn't going to, she finally spoke up.

"Did I say something wrong, Billy?"

"What? Oh, no, no Maggi, I just..." His voice trailed off.

"You just what?"

Billy tossed the last bite of cookie in a trashcan.

"Maggi, I don't know how to tell you this." His eyes were welling up; Maggi grabbed the sleeve of his shirt.

"Tell me what? Are you sick or something?"

"No, it's nothing like that. It's just that…well…everything we talked about, you know. My Uncle Max was going to make a few calls, and pretty soon St. Mary's story would be making national news."

Maggi just looked at him, her smile vanishing.

"It's not going to happen, Maggi."

She closed her eyes, and her cup of tea fell to the ground.

"He tried, Maggi, he really did. But no one–"

"You promised, Billy, you promised." Now it was Maggi's eyes that were filling with tears.

"I know, but–"

"There are no buts, Billy. Around here, a person's only as good as the promises he keeps. I don't know what passes for a backbone in Hollywood, but in Logansport, it's a whole lot more than you've got." She was now poking him in the chest, and her words came out between clenched teeth.

"Maggi, please…"

He was backing up now. "Don't give me please, either, Mr. Delaney. This is about the last thing I needed to hear. The Bishop's coming this Sunday to probably shut us down, and I was stupid enough to pin all my hopes on a washed-up actor with no possible skills or talents whatsoever." She turned, and waving her hand backward, walked toward the path out of the park.

Billy didn't even try to follow her. Her words cut through him, confirming in his mind every doubt he'd ever had about himself.

Luke Donahue took the stage, and introduced the first song of the next set.

"Ladies and gentlemen, as the band takes their seats and you take yours, I'd like to introduce our next number. It was recorded by a one-armed trumpet player named Joe "Wingy" Malone, and it's called

'Trying To Stop My Crying.'"
Billy had already reached the edge of the park, and was headed into town.

Chapter 28

"Come on, Jimmy, I think we've heard enough for tonight. Finish whatever that is you're drinking and let's head out."

Karl had no intention of staying for the second set of music from the jazz band. Even behind his sunglasses, Jimmy could tell he was serious.

Grace Wilson had taken up her position behind the table near where Karl and Jimmy were standing. As the 'Queen' of the Red Hat Society chapter, she supervised the filling of the Dixie cups and anything else that was required. She heard Karl's "whatever that is" comment, but said nothing. Why be as rude as that out-of-towner? Still, she bristled at the thought that someone didn't like her tea.

"Hi, Peach." Ernie had snuck up behind her, kissing her on her neck. "You ready to head back to our seats?"

"Sure, honey. I just need to wait for these last few cups." She nodded towards Karl and Jimmy across the table.

"What? Oh…" Ernie rolled his eyes as he recognized the two.

Jimmy held his cup over towards Grace, who filled it with the last of the pitcher's tea. She set the empty pitcher down and walked a few feet to gather some others.

"Oh, for God's sake, Dozan, what are you, a sponge?" Karl didn't notice Ernie behind the table. Jimmy responded in kind, forgetting the Jenkins and Hundley routine.

"Sorry, Mr. Schwarz, but I don't see what the hurry is for. We're not going to announce the deal with St. Mary's and the diocese for a few more days. After that, it'll be a few months until we turn it into a restaurant…"

"Look, you little twit. I have absolutely no intention of turning that decrepit old church into a restaurant. Once the Bishop announces the sale and the papers are all signed, that place is coming down, brick by brick. A small price to pay for this town kicking me out on my–"

"You...you...I KNEW IT!"

Karl spun around, facing Ernie.

Ernie was pointing right at Karl's face. "I knew there was something familiar about you. Mr. Jenkins, my Aunt Fannie." Ernie's finger was shaking. And soon, his whole hand.

"Hey, easy there, grandpa, I don't know what you're–"

Ernie's left arm had now curled up around his chest, and he was no longer looking right into Karl's eyes, but almost through him. His entire body was vibrating now, and he began slumping forward.

"Ernie? ERNIE!" Grace had heard him shout, and was coming back to the table. As she reached him, he slumped forward, sprawling across the red, white and blue cloth.

Jimmy dropped his cup into the grass. A few people had jogged over to the table now. Someone yelled for Dr. Billings, who was up front near the band shell. He bolted out of his seat and ran back to the table. Karl backed away, pulling Jimmy with him.

A few men gently pulled Ernie from the table and laid him in the grass. Grace softly brushed the wisps of white hair from his forehead, and then kissed him.

"Don't you dare, old man, don't you dare," she whispered.

Chapter 29

The streets of Logansport were nearly deserted, with everyone still at the jazz concert. Billy walked down Main, his hands clenched deep in the pockets of his jacket. At the corner of Lincoln and Main, he could hear the yellow caution streetlight clicking overhead.

He turned the corner, not really sure where he was headed, but so depressed he didn't care. It was now dark; he soon found himself standing under a spotlight over a building's entryway.

"Schwarz and Kelly," he read from the engraved concrete above the light. A bronze plaque next to the door caught his eye.

This plaque is dedicated to Gerhard Schwarz and Seamus Kelly, two of Logansport's founding fathers. Without their selfless devotion and unwavering philanthropy, Logansport would not be the 'Gem of the Midwest' she is today. They are truly inspirations for generations to come, and we are eternally grateful. Erected this day, April 8, 1959, under my hand, Mayor Hampton Kidd Barker, and the Logansport Town Council.

Billy put his hand up on the plaque, directly over Seamus Kelly's name. "Kelly. That's a coincidence," he said out loud.

"Not really. He was my great-grandfather."

Billy turned, and saw Maggi standing a few feet from him near the curb.

"And he never broke a promise." She turned and headed back to Main Street.

"Maggi, wait." Billy jogged over to her, taking her by the arm.

"Billy, I'm sorry for storming off like that at the concert, really I am. But I've wasted a couple of days already, and I don't have much time left. Honestly, I appreciate your coming here, but I've got to–"

"Maggi, I wasn't just blowing smoke today. I really thought we could get some national exposure for St. Mary's. Max was on the phone all day, Maggi, but–"

"–but no one in the main stream media cares about the troubles of some little church out here in Podunkville, right, Billy?"

"No, Maggi. No one cares about a washed-up actor with no skills or talents whatsoever." He relaxed his grip on Maggi's arm. "I'm sorry again, Maggi." Billy backed off, turned and headed up Lincoln.

This time it was Maggi who ran after Billy.

"Billy, I didn't mean what I said back at the concert."

"Yeah, right."

"It's just that I'm so fed-up with other people, outsiders, making decisions that affect my life, the lives of the kids in my choir, their parents, and everyone else at St. Mary's. Then you come along, another outsider, with grand promises to make things better. Can you blame me for feeling let down?"

"And I suppose you understand what it's like to be somebody who has everything done for them day after day, week after week, year after year, and then one day you wake up and realize that you're a nobody with nothing to offer. Uncle Max told me once that he's a nobody, and that nobodies just blend into the sidewalk. Any clue what that feels like, Maggi? I don't think so. Still, I decide to go out and try to figure out where my life is going to lead me, and instead I end up here with an empty hand."

Maggi looked down at the sidewalk, then back up at Billy.

"No, Mr. Delaney, I'm not a somebody like you once were. Nobody's ever done anything for me day after day, week after week, year after year. When I was a little girl, my daddy taught me a little saying: 'If it's meant to be, it is up to me and thee.' In other words, God will hold my hand, but he'll never take me anywhere, just show me the way and if I take him with me, I'll be safe and happy. Everything I have in life, a father who loves me, the children's choir, a home, and a church are because I chose to accept them and God into my life. And now, someone wants to take part of that away from me, and I can't feel God's hand in mine right now." She was sobbing now, and Billy put his hands on her shoulder, pulling her into him.

"Hey, hey," he said. "It's all right, Maggi." He brushed her hair from her eyes. "As far as I'm concerned, you've always been a somebody. I'm the one who never realized I was depending on all the wrong people."

They stood there together on the silent street for a few moments. When the ambulance from County General rounded the corner of Lincoln and raced past them, its lights were on but no siren blared from its roof.

Chapter 30

"St. Mary's...corn...St. Mary's...corn...corn..." It was barely a whisper, but Grace could hear him, she was that close.

The ambulance kicked up gravel as it pulled onto Route 47 for the three-mile ride to County General in Paxton Township.

"How ya doin', Mr. Wilson?" The paramedic, a stout young man named Henry, kept an eye on the blood pressure readout. He picked up a two-way radio. "Ninety-two over sixty, General. ETA in two."

"ETA in two, copy," came the crackling response.

"Corn...cone." Ernie opened his eyes for the first time since the park. They darted around the interior of the ambulance, finally finding Grace's loving gaze. She saw something on his face she hadn't seen in years.

Fear.

"Shhh, sweetie, we're almost there." She patted his forehead with a small towel, wiping away beads of sweat despite the coolness of the interior of the ambulance. His eyes followed her closely until the tears forced him to close them again. A single drop ran down each side of his face.

"St....Mary's...cone."

* * *

Billy and Maggi walked the dark streets of Logansport aimlessly for nearly an hour that night. And in that time, he was able to tell her most of his life's story, from the early days growing up with stage parents who took him on every conceivable audition in Southern

California to his years on television, then the deception by those same parents and his uncle coming to his aide.

There wasn't much to tell about his teenage years; he only knew auditions, but grew increasingly tired of the rejections for anything worthwhile. Still, he never let on to Max, who always seemed to say the right thing or do the right thing, keeping Billy's outlook positive.

Maggi listened intently to it all. When he finally let his voice trail off, she instinctively reached out and took his hand.

"I guess we're not all that different, then, are we?" she said.

"What do you mean?"

"Oh, you know, up until a few years ago, I thought my life was pretty great too. Did I tell you I had just been accepted to DePaul University a few weeks before…"

"Before your mom?"

"Yeah. But then that happened, and Daddy lost his job, and I guess things just got away from us. I was going to major in vocal performance, maybe even sing with a philharmonic choir some day. Still, I've always had St. Mary's, and when Father Bob gave me the part-time job in the rectory, and I took over as the kid's choir director, life seemed to kind of settle in, you know what I mean? Now, the diocese has decided money is more important…" She sighed.

"Well, you know what the vacuum cleaner salesman said, don't you?"

"No, what?"

"Sucks, doesn't it?"

She groaned. "Please don't tell me you're considering standup, Billy."

It was the first time he'd seen her smile since the barbecue.

"Listen, Maggi, there's something I've been meaning to tell you. I'm not sure I'm the ideal person to understand what you've been going through at St. Mary's anyway. You see, I–"

She put her hand over his mouth.

"I don't want to talk about St. Mary's anymore tonight, Billy. As far as I'm concerned, it's in God's hands." Billy held his hands up as if to say 'I surrender,' and said no more.

They walked another half-block, and found themselves in front of Maggi's house. The lights were on in the living room, and they could see two people standing on the porch.

"That's my dad," she said, "but I don't recognize the other man."

"I do. It's my Uncle Max."

Patrick and Max stepped off the porch and met them halfway up the walk.

"Hey, kiddo," Max said. "We've been looking for you two."

"Maggi and I were working some things out."

"Hi, Daddy. What's up?" She reached up and kissed her father on his cheek.

"Maggi, it's Ernie Wilson."

Maggi tried to read the tone of his voice. She didn't want to hear what she heard, and put her hands over her mouth.

"Oh, no, he didn't..."

"No, he didn't, but he's over at County General. Father Bob left about twenty minutes ago. From what he told me, it sounds like a stroke. Grace is there, and Father thought you might like to stop by to sit with her."

"Of course, of course." She patted the pockets of her denim jacket. "I think I left my keys inside. I'll just–"

Patrick jingled them in his hand. "C'mon, I'll take you."

She looked at Billy, who in turn looked at Max.

"Would you all mind if Billy and I rode along?"

"We'd appreciate it, Max," said Patrick. The four walked quickly across the lawn and climbed into Patrick's Dodge Caravan.

He turned the key, and the stereo came to life.

"Good evening, Logansport, Dan Driscoll back in the studio after the abbreviated jazz concert tonight. Most of you were at the park, but for those of you who weren't, our very own Ernie Wilson of the Ben Franklin was taken to County General this evening. I don't have any details yet, but I'll keep you up-to-date as I hear any news. Until then, let's listen to Miss Victoria Spivey, and her wonderful blues rendition of "Grow Old Together."

Chapter 31

They found Grace sitting in a day room on the third floor. She was facing a television as it played an old movie, but she was clearly paying no attention. Patrick found the remote and powered it off.

Billy and Max grabbed the two chairs on either side of the television across from Grace, and Patrick stood near the door.

Maggi sat next to Grace on the cloth sofa, and pulled a tissue from the box on the coffee table and offered it to her.

Grace sniffled. "Thank you, dear."

"The nurse said Ernie's sleeping right now, so we didn't want to disturb him," Maggi said.

"Yes. Father Bob's in with him. I just couldn't bear those machines beeping and blinking in the dark. He looked so small in that bed, too."

"What's the doctor say, Mrs. Wilson?" Billy asked.

Grace dabbed at the corner of her eye with the tissue. "Oh, you know, a lot of medical terms we'll never understand or remember, but basically Ernie's had a small stroke. We won't know how severe until tomorrow morning. Right now, he can only say a few words, but he was able to squeeze my hand pretty hard as they wheeled him down the hall."

"I'm sure some of the few words are 'I love you', right?"

Grace gave a little laugh. "Well, you'd think, huh? No, he kept saying 'St. Mary's' over and over. Sometimes I think he loves that building more than me. Anyway, that's why Father Bob's in there, I thought that's what Ernie was asking for."

"I'm sure it was, Grace," Patrick said from behind her. "You know he loves you, and we all love him. I think that's going to get him through." He put his hands on her shoulders; she patted his left hand in return.

"Thank you for coming, Patrick. You know what else that old man is talking about? The Sweet Corn Festival! Of all things...of course, it's coming out as corn-cone, but I'm sure he's upset that he's going to miss it. We've been to every one, you know."

Someone knocked on the door to the day room. Father Bob leaned in to the room.

"Mind if I join you all?" he said.

Max stood up from his chair and ushered Father Bob into it.

"Well," he continued, "he finally drifted off to sleep a few minutes ago. Tough old bird, you know?"

"Thank you so much for coming, Father," Grace said.

"Oh, Grace, you know I'd be here even if you hadn't called. You were right, though. He kept saying 'St. Mary's' over and over when I came in, with a few corn-cones thrown in."

Grace looked at Maggi. "See, I told you! St. Mary's and that corn festival. As soon as he's better, he's going to get such a scolding..." Her voice trailed off, and Maggi gave her a gentle hug.

"Maggi, I'm sorry to bring this up right now, but I'll need you to finish up those records in the basement sometime tomorrow. The Bishop wants to go through them on Sunday afternoon."

"Sure, Father, I wasn't planning on going to the Sweet Corn Festival anyway. After lunch okay with you?"

"Absolutely, Maggi, anytime. I'm coming back over here in the morning, and then I'll see you in the rectory in the afternoon."

"I'll help you with the records, Maggi," Billy said. She nodded back at him.

Father Bob stood up and shook everyone's hand, thanking them for coming.

"Grace, I want you to go home and get some sleep, and I'll meet you back here after eight in the morning. Patrick, would you be so kind as to drive her home?"

"Not a problem."

"Thank you, and thanks to all of you again for coming. I need to stop downstairs in the chapel, so I'll say goodnight."

"Goodnight, Father," they all said in unison.

When he had disappeared down the hallway to the elevator, Grace finally stood from the sofa.

"I'm just going to go peek at him one more time," she said. "I can't remember the last time we spent an evening apart."

"Take your time, Grace, we'll wait right here," Maggi said.

After she was gone, Maggi said, "Anyone know what exactly happened? What was he doing when this happened?"

"We're not sure, honey. When Max and I got to the table where he was, there was a pretty good crowd standing around already. Except, of course, those two fellas staying out at Bea and Al's. I saw them walking out of the park as if nothing was happening. Some people..." Patrick said, shaking his head.

"Maybe we'll have a chance to chat with our fellow boarders," Max said.

"Don't worry about it, Max. If they can walk away like that, they probably couldn't care less what decent people like you and Billy would have to say."

"Yeah, I suppose your right. Still..."

Grace stepped back into the day room. "Shall we go?" she said.

Max offered his arm, Grace accepted, and they all walked out of the room and into the night.

Chapter 32

Beatrice picked up the extension in the kitchen on its second ring, forgetting to wipe the pancake batter off of her hands.
"Good morning, Bea and Al's Bed and Breakfast, can I help you?"
"Uh, good morning, I'm looking for a Mr. Max Duncan."
"Well, I don't know if he's up yet, we had quite a night around here, but I can go check for you. Who can I say is calling?"
"My name's Art Paulsen. I'm returning his call from yesterday."
"Okay, I'll–did you say Art Paulsen?"
"Yes, ma'am."
"As in syndicated columnist Art Paulsen?"
"Guilty as charged."
"Hang on a sec. AL!"
"What now?" Al called back from the dining room.
"Have you seen Max? He's got a call...Art Paulsen, the newspaper guy from the Sun-Times."
"Yeah, he's–"
The kitchen door flew inward as Max raced over to Bea. He grabbed the phone from her hand, looked skyward and whispered, "Thank you!" and then placed it against his ear.
"Art, my friend, how are ya?"
"Max, I thought that was your voice on my answering machine. Sorry I didn't get back to you sooner, I was under a deadline last night. What can I do for you? Wait, before you answer that, why am I calling a bed and breakfast in an Illinois area code?"
Max put his hand over the receiver. "Bea, I don't want to be in your way here. Is there another phone where I can take this?"

She tore a paper towel from the roller and wiped the pancake batter from Max's cheek. "Sure, sweetie, out in the front room by the desk. I'll hang this up for you."

He kissed her on the cheek. "It's Art Paulsen!" he said, and ran out of the kitchen.

Bea listened until she heard Max pick up, and then she hung up her phone.

* * *

"Jimmy?" Karl rapped lightly on the door of the room next to his.

"Jimmy?"

No answer. Jimmy had left an hour before breakfast. Dan Driscoll was rolling down the driveway on his way to pick up some equipment from the station for the remote broadcast at the Sweet Corn Festival, when he saw Jimmy step off of the porch. Dan waved, but Jimmy never looked up.

Karl opened the door to Jimmy's room. It was surprisingly neat; for a moment, Karl thought Jimmy had checked out until he saw the suitcase on the stand next to the dresser.

I never should have told him, Karl thought. *Muscle-head can barely walk and chew gum, and I tell him my plan for that church.*

Karl saw the folded piece of paper on the dresser with the word 'Boss' written on top.

Uh-oh.

> Mister S.–last night with that old guy has really got me bugged. He acted like he knew you, then he keeled over. And that was right after you told me about St. Mary's, which is different than what you told the Bishop. I've got to get out of here for a while, boss. Something just don't feel right–Jimmy

Doesn't, dimwit, doesn't.

Karl crumpled the letter and threw it against the wall next to the bed.

"Keep walking, Dozan," he said out loud. He pulled the gold money clip from his pants pocket, peeled off a hundred dollar bill, and dropped it into the suitcase.

"Severance."

Chapter 33

Maggi pulled into Bea and Al's driveway a little after eight o'clock. A light mist from the overcast skies only served to further depress her; she didn't even bother with an umbrella.

Lawn chairs still littered the lawn from the previous day's barbecue. She absent-mindedly folded two of them and leaned them against the steps of the front porch and went inside.

The tiny bell atop the inside of the door caused Max to turn around, phone in hand. Standing at the front desk, he smiled and waved at Maggi, then turned back to his conversation.

A side door in the hallway opened, and Al emerged from the basement, black soot across his face.

"Four hundred year old furnace…no heat in this place since '99…I could burn the house down, and it still wouldn't light off…piece of–" Al finally looked up. "Maggi!" He held out a blackened hand, but quickly pulled it back.

"Hi, Al."

He pulled a rag out of his back pocket and tried to wipe his hands. "Sorry about that, kiddo. What brings you by here on such a miserable morning?"

"I'm supposed to pick up Billy Delaney. We're heading over to County to see how Ernie's doing."

"Oh, yeah, I couldn't believe that happened. I imagine Grace is taking it pretty hard."

"She is. If anything, we'll just be there for her, you know?"

"Sure, sure. Listen, you give her a hug from us, okay?"

Maggi nodded.

"Let me see if I can roust the boy. Hang on, Maggi." Al bounded up the stairs.

Maggi walked back into the parlor, where Max was still on the phone. She didn't want to appear to be eavesdropping, so she walked to the far corner near a tall window to watch the falling leaves. Still, Max's voice carried throughout the first floor.

"Art, that's terrific news...no, Billy's upstairs...yeah, right off Route 47, that's it. I'll look for you around four o'clock. Take care, Art. Bye." Max hung up the phone as Billy came down the stairs. Maggi turned from the window, catching his eye.

"Glad you could join us, Mr. Delaney," Max said. "I'm sure Bea saved a few pancakes for you; how about it, Maggi? Care to join us? Besides, I've got some things we need to discuss."

Billy never took his eyes off Maggi. He walked over to her and gave her a brief hug; somehow, he sensed she needed it.

"I'm not really hungry, Maxie," Billy said.

"Thanks, Mr. Duncan, but no, we really need to get to the hospital. Grace and Father Bob are already there."

Max came over to the two young people and said, "All right, you better get going, then. And I thought I told you to call me Uncle Max, young lady."

"And I thought I told you never to call me late for breakfast, Max," Billy said, smiling. "Come on, Maggi. Oh, don't forget I'm going to St. Mary's with Maggi to help with those boxes afterwards, Max."

"Okay, kids. Drive safe, it looks a little slick out there." Maggi and Billy walked out the front door and down to the driveway.

Max watched the minivan disappear down Locust.

Art Paulsen, please don't be late. You've got a deadline.

Chapter 34

Maggi and Billy walked past the nurse's station on the third floor as Grace was coming out of Ernie's room. The hospital barely resembled the quiet, hushed building of the previous evening. Medical personnel popped in and out of various rooms, as well as other early morning visitors to loved ones.

Grace greeted each of them with a hug. Her eyes were red; she admitted to very little sleep and very many tears. "When Ernie doesn't get enough sleep, I always tell him his eyes look like two burned holes in a blanket," she said.

Billy offered to get her a cup of coffee, and she accepted.

"How's he doing, Grace?" Maggi asked.

"Well…" she paused for a second. "Father Bob's in with him right now. Ernie woke up a few minutes ago, and when he saw Father, he tried to sit up! Of all the stubborn…anyway, he got very agitated, and started in with that 'St. Mary's, corn-cone' business. Over and over, he just wouldn't stop. Finally, Father Bob told him he'd bring him some corn from the festival when he could, but that didn't seem to matter to Ernie. He finally pounded the bed with his fist and closed his eyes."

Billy returned with the coffee and handed it to Grace.

"Should we go in and see him?" Maggi asked.

"I think he'd like that, sweetheart."

Maggi and Billy walked down the hall and stood in the doorway of room 312. The curtains were drawn and the lights were off, and the other bed in the room lay empty. Father Bob was sitting on a brown felt chair with a cart full of electronic equipment between him and Ernie. He was reading something quietly to Ernie when he saw them. He stood, set the book on the bed, and walked to the door.

"Hi, kids, thanks for coming." He motioned for them to step back into the hallway.

"The doctor was in a few minutes ago. All he could say was that it was too early to know the extent of the damage from the stroke. If it's not too bad, with therapy he could be as good as new in a few months."

"Father, I know the Bishop is coming tomorrow...why don't you head back to the rectory, and we'll stay with Ernie for awhile," Maggi said.

"The Bishop...yes, I suppose I should. Odd, though, isn't it? With so much of that unpleasant business going on, I can't think of any place more important to be than right here. That man in there has been to mass every weekend save for one since that church opened. How many different pastors? How many midnight Christmas masses? How many times did that lovely woman down the hall put on her finest hat and have Ernie escort her up the aisle at Easter? And now, he's probably going to miss the final mass. He never gave up on St. Mary's, but I feel like the church gave up on him."

Maggi didn't know what to say.

"We'll take over for a little while, Father," Billy said.

He nodded, patted Billy on the arm and walked down the hall to the elevator.

Billy followed Maggi into the room. Ernie's eyes fluttered a bit, then opened.

"Hi, Ernie, it's me Maggi. You remember Billy Delaney..."

Billy waved at Ernie, but then realized Ernie probably wasn't in much of a waving mood.

"St. Mary's..." Ernie said, clear as a bell.

"Yup, Father Bob had to head back there, he's got some things to attend to." Maggi patted his hand; Ernie closed his eyes at these words.

"Bish..." he whispered.

Maggi looked at Billy standing on the other side of the bed. "Yes, the Bishop's coming in tomorrow. But let's not-"

"Corn-cone."

"I know, Father's going to—"

"Corn-cone. St. Mary's."

Ernie lifted his right hand; an IV protruded from the back of it just below his wrist. He reached over to Billy and grabbed the sleeve of his jacket.

"Corn-cone. St. Mary's."

Billy looked helplessly at Maggi. It was then that she noticed the book at the foot of Ernie's bed; Father Bob had forgotten it when he left. Maggi picked it up.

It was Father Bob's own Bible, and it was opened to the Book of Matthew.

"Ernie, would you mind if I continued reading for Father Bob?"

Ernie let go of Billy's jacket, and closed his eyes. Almost imperceptive, he gave a single nod.

"But Jesus looked at them and said, 'What then is this that is written: The stone which the builders rejected, this has become the chief cornerstone'?"

"Excuse me, folks..."

Maggi looked at the doorway. A nurse was bringing in a small cart.

"It's time for a little housekeeping with Mr. Wilson. I'm afraid I'll have to let him have a little privacy and a few hours' sleep."

Maggi stepped close to Ernie, leaned in and gave him a kiss on the cheek.

"Get some rest, Ernie. We're going to need you back at the Ben Franklin."

"St. Mary's."

Maggi and Billy hurried into the hall; she quickly closed the door behind them before bursting into tears.

Chapter 35

The rain had turned steady in the short time they were in the hospital. Billy held his jacket over Maggi's head as they sprinted for the minivan. She hit the remote unlock button on her keychain, and the taillights flashed along with a double beep.

Once inside, Billy took the bible from Maggi and began thumbing through it.

"So what did that mean?" Billy asked.

"What did what mean?" Maggi turned the ignition key, and the minivan sparked to life.

"That little bit you read to Ernie inside, you know, about the stone being rejected."

"Oh, right." Maggi was checking her mirrors as she backed out of the lot. "Well, I've heard it most often explained this way: In Jesus' time, the Jews had been awaiting the coming of the Messiah for hundreds of years. Some were expecting a giant, some a regal, God-like deity. So when this simple son of a carpenter proclaimed that he was truly the Son of God, it was considered blasphemous by some people. And his message was so basic, so simple–love each other, and love God and give Him thanks for all that we have–that those in authority were convinced he wasn't the Messiah."

"So they crucified him. But you said, 'Jesus said to them...'."

Maggi smiled at Billy as the windshield wipers erased another film of rain.

"Billy, some day you've got to read that book. He knew everything that was to happen to him, saw every reason for every event that took place in the world around him. He would look into someone's eyes and read their heart, listen to their words and know their souls. He knew when he was speaking that some day he would be the cornerstone of the church we know today, despite his being rejected in his time."

"You got all of that from those few words?"

"That I did, Billy. With a little help from wonderful pastors like Father Bob and his homilies."

"From his what?"

"Homilies. You know, sermons. You're not Catholic, are you?"

"No, I–"

"Well, we call the sermon a homily. You know, at every mass we have readings from the Holy Scriptures. Then, Father gives a homily in which he relates those readings to his message for us. Except of course when he talks about money on Stewardship Sunday. Then, it's called a sermon."

The minivan was pulling into the gravel driveway between the rectory and St. Mary's.

"Here we are. Tell you what, Billy, why don't you head down to the basement in the church–the side door's open and the door to the basement is in back of the steps that lead to the old choir loft. I'm going to drop Father Bob's bible in his office."

"Okay, Maggi. Hey, you know what?"

"What?"

"I'd give anything to have your insight about stuff like what you just told me. You know, about Jesus and what he meant."

"And I'd like to take the credit for that insight, Billy, but all I did was open my heart and listen to him. At times when I thought he wasn't speaking to me, it was just that I wasn't listening. You've just got to listen. That's all there is to it."

As if on cue, the light rain pelting the windshield stopped.

Chapter 36

Father Bob emerged from the sacristy in the back of St. Mary's with an armload of bulletins. On the cover in large block letters it said 'Welcome Bishop Barnes' along with a cross draped in a cloth. He set a stack on either side of the doors, and then straightened a couple of hymnals on the cart. The baptismal font sat motionless; he walked over and checked the water level. That was when he first heard it.

Someone was crying. They were soft sobs, the kind you hear from an audience at a sad movie. Father Bob scanned the pews; over on the left side about halfway up, he saw a lone figure, rocking back and forth on the kneeler.

Father Bob went around the back of the pews and up the side aisle. As he came closer, the person stood. Father Bob went a row ahead of him and turned to face him. It was a rather large man with his hands buried in his face; still, he didn't recognize him.

"Can I help you, son?"

The man pulled his hands away; he reached into his back pocket and pulled out a handkerchief, then loudly cleared his sinuses.

"I seriously doubt it, Father. I think I've sinned big time."

"Are you Catholic? Would you like me to hear your confession?"

The man sat back down in the pew; Father Bob did the same two rows ahead of him.

"Oh, I'm Catholic, all right, but I haven't been to mass in years. That's part of the problem."

"Believe it or not, it doesn't really matter to me when you last went to church, but that you're here now. And from what I can tell, you really need to talk."

The man looked upward towards one of the plaques beneath a massive stained glass window. In the scene, he could see an image of Jesus prostrate on the ground as a woman gently wipes his face with a cloth.

"Veronica..." he said softly.

Father Bob looked at the window and then back at the man. "You haven't been away that long, friend. A lot of Catholics couldn't tell me her name if I begged them."

"She had courage, didn't she?"

"How do you mean?"

"Here's this crowd screaming and cursing at this man, yelling for him to be executed, and out she steps to give him a little comfort. She didn't care what the others thought, she didn't care what could possibly happen to her, she knew in her heart how to do the right thing when it was called for."

"Yes, I suppose you're right, son."

The man looked at Father Bob.

"Do you have an office where we could talk? You might want to take some notes."

* * *

Billy pulled the string on the light bulb hanging near the center of the basement. The stone foundation walls shimmered as condensation had formed on them overnight. At first, the musty smell was almost too much for him. He soon grew used to it, though, as he moved some empty boxes to a single pile off to one side.

He could tell where Maggi had been working. The empty boxes were all labeled 'Church records' followed by the dates of the contents. She had nearly finished; the only full box on the shelf was labeled 1921-1930. Billy pulled it off the shelf, but the bottom was not sealed and the contents spilled out over the floor.

"Oh, crud," he said.

Yellowed envelopes bulging with papers were scattered

everywhere. He refolded the bottom of the box, and began picking up each envelope and setting it inside.
Membership directories.
Knights of Columbus meeting minutes.
Baptismal certificates.
Weddings.
Funerals.
Paid bills.
Cornerstone contents.

Billy held this last one in his hands. Maggi had shown Billy the cornerstone of St. Mary's during their walk after the jazz concert, and had told him how she used to sit near it as a little girl and trace the engraved date, 1921, with her finger.

But contents? Billy always thought they were solid stones, he had no idea they actually put things in them.

He pulled back the brittle flap from the envelope and pulled out a crumbling piece of paper.

"The Parish and people of St. Mary's of Logansport, Illinois," he began reading aloud, "have been the proud recipient of many kind and generous gifts prior to her dedication on September 24, 1921. It is the wish of the faithful that this record be drawn declaring the contents of the cornerstone as a record for future generations. It is the further wish of the faithful that those future generations will understand what sacrifices were made to build this house, the house of the Lord."

Billy gently turned over the piece of paper.

Cornerstone contents, he now read to himself.

Silver dollar and various coins to begin rebuilding fund should disaster strike, given by Susan Crohan, Logansport Librarian.

Grand Army of the Republic Medal, Post 14, from Raphael Stimpson, Civil War Veteran.

Logansport Lookout Newspaper, March 15, 1921.

Tin box containing cash donations, stock certificates, personal letters and other gifts from parishioners of St. Mary's.

Letter from Mr. Louis C. Tiffany, including stained glass window

inventory and certificate of authenticity.
   Roll of all registered parishioners of St. Mary's, including children.
   Billy dropped the letter and bolted upright.
   Cash donations? Stock certificates? St. Mary's corn-cone?
   "WOOHOO!!" he screamed, punching his fist into the air.
   "Billy, you scared the daylights out of me." Maggi was coming down the stairs. "What are you screaming about?"
   He ran over and grabbed her hands, and as best he could do, danced her in a circle.
   "You won't believe what I've found," he said as they stopped spinning.
   He picked up the letter, and after reading the front to her, turned it over and showed her the contents list.
   "Cash and stock, Maggi. Cash and stock! This is what Ernie has been trying to tell us. He must have remembered what was put in the cornerstone, but had the stroke before he could tell us."
   "Oh, Billy, how much cash could they have put in there? Remember, this was a small town even then, and we didn't have the kind of money we need now to just hide in tin boxes for 'someday.'"
   "I know, Maggi, but stock certificates. I'm willing to bet that there are shares of stock in there that have split and doubled and grown a thousand fold over the years. I know I'm right, I can just feel it! For once, Maggi, I feel it."
   She looked deep into his eyes. "You really do, don't you? All right, let's go show Father Bob. But I really don't think he'll like the idea of someone breaking open the cornerstone of the church."
   "You let me worry about that. I think I know how we can do it so no one will be able to tell."

Chapter 37

Maggi and Billy burst through the door of the rectory. "Father Bob?" Maggi shouted as they looked in every room on the first floor.

Finally making their way to the kitchen in the rear of the building, they found him. He was sitting at the old Formica table, his hands behind his head. No expression graced his face, and his eyes were closed. A kettle on the stove steamed from the spout, and the smell of brewed tea filled the hallway.

They went into the kitchen, only to find another man sitting across from Father Bob at the table.

"Hi, kids." He closed his eyes again. The other man just nodded at them and sipped his tea.

"Oh, pardon me, where are my manners? Maggi, this is Jimmy Dozan. Jimmy, Maggi Kelly. And I think Jimmy's met Billy Delaney here."

"Yeah, you're staying out at Bea's with that other guy, right?"

Jimmy looked at his cup. "Let's just say we had rooms next to each other."

Maggi put the cornerstone contents list in front of Father Bob.

He picked it up, read the front, and said, "How nice, Maggi. Maybe now when they tear down St. Mary's, we'll have something to put in the glass case over at the library."

"Tear it down?" Maggi said incredulously. "Why would they tear it down? I've heard of churches closing, but they never tear them down."

"I guess there's a first for everything."

Everyone looked at Jimmy.

"What do you mean?" Billy asked.

"I'm sorry to bring such bad news to you all, but that guy I'm with isn't what he says he is. He's bought the building, and had told the Bishop that he was going to turn it into a restaurant, but I found out last night he's just going to tear it down out of spite for this little town."

Maggi burst into tears again, as Billy hugged her.

"Father Bob," Billy said, "we found this list in the basement with the other records. I really believe there might be some stocks and things in there that might be worth something, maybe even enough to save St. Mary's."

"It doesn't matter anymore, Billy. The diocese sold the building–"

"It does matter, Father. Unless the diocese signed the papers, maybe we can convince Bishop Barnes to give us a reprieve. We'd like your permission to open up the cornerstone. Tonight."

Father Bob looked at Jimmy. "Did your boss sign the papers?"

"No, they were going to wait until just after mass tomorrow. We came to town a few days ago to make sure something like this didn't happen to kill the deal. But I'll tell you what, my boss is a pretty hard man. I doubt if anything can stop him now."

"How are you going to get into the cornerstone? I can't have you taking a sledgehammer and pounding away out there, it just wouldn't be safe," Father Bob said, turning to Maggi and Billy.

"Father, Maggi showed me the cornerstone's location just now. The backside of it is inside the coat closet. If we go in that way, I'm sure we can get to it without harming the exterior."

Father Bob looked around the two of them. "Maggi, what do you think?"

Maggi wiped her eyes. "I don't know, I don't know. But after hearing what he just told us, I don't see how it could hurt."

Billy looked at her. "C'mon, Maggi, let's go get those stocks." They turned to walk out of the kitchen.

"Hey!" It was Jimmy. "Could you use a little muscle?"

Chapter 38

"This is Father Santos, may I help you?"

Karl pressed the cell phone next to his ear. "Evening, Father Santos, Karl Schwarz. I just wanted to make sure everything was still on for tomorrow. I plan on meeting the Bishop right after mass at St. Mary's."

"Yes, Mr. Schwarz, the Bishop has finished up his message to the people of Logansport, and we will probably want to depart the area as soon as possible."

"Good, good. Tell you what, they have a little rectory right next door, let's meet there. I'm anxious to get this thing done."

"I have no doubt you are. What time will you be arriving in Logansport?"

"Oh, uh, I came down a couple of days early, wanted to take a trip down memory lane, if you know what I mean."

"Pleasant memories?"

"Oh, nothing but..."

"Listen, Mr. Schwarz, I just wanted you to know that I haven't been in favor of your plan from its inception. But the council has spoken, and I'm merely the Bishop's aide."

"Just so long as the council has spoken, then I suppose we have nothing more to say about it."

"I suppose we don't."

"Then you'll ensure the Bishop has the papers?"

"Yes, I–"

Karl slapped his cell phone shut, disconnecting the call.

Peons, he thought.

Chapter 39

Maggi and Jimmy stood outside the coat closet, waiting for Billy to return from Bea and Al's with the tools. The overcast sky was now darkening as night began to fall.

"He really hates us that much, that he'd do that to this town?"

"Yeah, I'm sorry to say. I guess his old man was some big shot in this town way back when. He kicked him out after high school, told him to go make it on his own. Boy, he did, all right. Then, the old man kicks, right? Boss doesn't get a dime, says it all went to the town. That's why he's doin' this."

"What a jerk. It's always about money, isn't it? I'm just so sick of it. And here we are, about to tear apart a closet, and why? Because of money. Money's either going to tear this place down or keep it alive."

"I'm really sorry, Maggi. I didn't find out about it until last night at that concert. We were talkin'—me and my boss—when this old guy starts goin' off on him, then keels over."

"Ernie."

"Beats me. Anyway, it was like a light went off in my head. I didn't want to work for this guy anymore. We've spent a lot of time walking around Logansport, you know, and it reminds me of my hometown. So this morning I take off, gonna figure out my next move; next thing I know, I end up here sittin' in one of the pews, rememberin' how happy I was as a kid. Next thing I know, I'm bawlin' like a baby and Father Bob's listening to me spill my guts about this whole thing."

Maggi looked away from Jimmy. "Lucky for you Father Bob can grant forgiveness. I'm not so sure about the rest of the town."

The front doors of the church swung open, and Billy entered carrying a sledgehammer in one hand and a shovel in the other.

"Sorry I'm late, guys. I brought a little help, though."

Behind Billy entered Max and another man they didn't recognize, both carrying buckets.

"This is my Uncle Max and his friend, Art Paulsen." Jimmy shook both their hands.

Maggi looked at Art. "You mean Art Paulsen of the Chicago Sun-Times?"

Art smiled. "And 315 other papers across the country. You must be Maggi. When Max here called me, I remembered a letter someone named Maggi sent to us about a church that was going to close. Thought I'd come down and do a column about it; didn't know I'd get to help tear it down."

"Hey, you kids better get moving," Max said. "Art and I will carry out the debris."

"Yeah," Art said. "I always wanted to add vandalism to my resume."

* * *

Billy and Jimmy took turns pounding at the plaster in the closet. As they would pull it away, Maggi would load it into a bucket and hand it to Max or Art, who would remove it to the dumpster behind the church.

By 8:30, they had found the wall. Billy was now like a man possessed; when Jimmy pointed this out to him, he replied that he was probably in the right building for that.

The top of the cornerstone peaked up about six inches from the floor of the closet. They could see a line running parallel along the top of the stone; Billy concluded that a section must have been removed in order to create a hollow for the documents and other contents.

Jimmy took a couple of swings with the sledgehammer, but struck above the line each time.

"Let me give it a shot," Billy said. He slid the hammer along the floor so that it struck just below the line. Compared to Jimmy's strikes, Billy's had a pop that sounded a little hollower. They looked at one another.

"This time, kiddo," Max said.

Billy nodded. He glanced at Maggi and winked. She smiled back at him.

POW!

The head of the sledgehammer broke through the back of the cornerstone. Dust sprayed outward into the closet as the five cheered. Billy pulled the hammer back out and tossed it aside.

"Well? You've come this far, kiddo, reach in there and see what you've found." Max gave Billy a little push on the shoulder.

Billy lay on the floor and stretched his arm deep into the hole. At first, he couldn't feel anything, but then realized he had to reach down as well. His hand found a metal object. It was square; he felt around a little more and found a handle.

"I got it!" he yelled.

As he backed his arm out of the hole, his pants, shirt and face were covered with dust. He swung it out into the middle of the floor as everyone crammed into the little room.

"This is it, Maggi," Billy said.

He turned a small latch on the front, and the lid popped open a bit. Billy lifted it back all the way, revealing stacks of folded envelopes.

Billy picked up the first, and noting the contents, handed it upwards. Max took the first envelope.

"Registered Parishioners of St. Mary's, 1921," he read.

Billy held up the next, which Jimmy took.

"Grand Army of the Republic Medal and Chapter Minutes."

Art Paulsen reached for the next.

"To the parishioners of St. Mary's and the people of Logansport. L. C. Tiffany."

Billy found a thick yellow envelope at the bottom of the tin box.

"Cash and stock certificates, courtesy of our parishioners." Billy gave it to Maggi. "Here, I think you should open it."

She took it from Billy, and they walked back out into the narthex of the church. She clicked on an overhead light and set the envelope on the table. She gently unwound the string sealing the flap to the envelope. Maggi lifted the bottom of the envelope, and the contents spilled out onto the table.

A few coins rolled to the floor; Billy separated the folding money from the other papers and began counting.

"Thirty-seven dollars and sixty-five cents," he said dejectedly.

"I told you we didn't have a lot of cash in those days." Maggi picked up the other papers; there were four envelopes, each labeled Stock Certificate.

She carefully opened each one and set the stock certificates on the table. Billy, Max and Jimmy thumbed through the other items in the box.

"Oh...my God," she said.

Billy stepped over to the table. "What is it, Maggi?"

"Altogether, it's nearly a thousand shares of the Logansport State Bank."

"A thousand! A THOUSAND!" Billy jumped in the air. "Maxie! It's a thousand shares of a bank!"

Max slapped him on the back. "Nice job, kiddo."

Maggi slapped Billy with a handful of the certificates.

"Didn't you hear me?" she said. "The Logansport State Bank. You've seen it. It's that big white building with the pillars across from the post office on Main. The one that has the Joe Picasso ceramic studio throughout the first floor?"

"What do you—"

"The Logansport State Bank closed in 1930, along with half the other banks in this country during the Depression, Billy. But unlike St. Mary's, we couldn't bear to tear down a fine building like a bank. We've just rented it out ever since." She threw the papers to the ground, where they scattered in all directions. "I knew it," she sighed.

Billy looked at Max.

Aw, geez, kiddo, Max thought.

"Maggi, I..." Billy just threw up his hands, unable to find any words that would help.

Art Paulsen stepped into the narthex from the coat closet. "Um, excuse me, folks, but I think you might want to read this."

Chapter 40

"Good Sunday morning, Logansport, this as always is Dan Driscoll on WLGP, AM-610. I just want to tell you what a great time we all had at the Sweet Corn Festival out at the fairgrounds yesterday. As is tradition, I have extreme sunburn and a bit of a raspy voice from having to do the entire eight-hour shift by myself, but that may be about to change.

"Myrna Fielding just dropped off my *Logansport Lookout*, so after a little news, we'll go through a list of the winners in the 4-H competition from yesterday.

"I also want to express a warm Logansport welcome to Bishop Barnes from the Diocese of Kankakee. He's here to make a little announcement at mass this morning over at St. Mary's, so if you haven't been for awhile, you've still got time to get over there. I don't think you'll want to miss it.

"Turning to the news, Randall Gibbels of the Post Office and Rosalie Drangle surprised everyone by announcing their engagement right after getting off of the Tilt-a-Whirl..."

* * *

Billy and Max arrived with Bea and Al at 10:00 that Sunday morning, a full half-hour before it was to begin. Bea had told them that whenever the Bishop comes, it is always filled, and considering the sadness over the inevitable news today, they should probably get there early.

They found room in a middle row of pews on the right side of the church. Billy looked around, and after a moment excused himself and walked to the choir area.

Maggi was passing out sheet music to the children who had already arrived.

"Need any help?"

Maggi turned. "Billy! Kids, I'd like you to meet a friend of mine, his name is Billy."

"Hi, Billy!" they all chimed.

"I'm sorry, I meant to introduce you to them the other night at the concert, but, well…"

"That's okay, Maggi, I understand."

"This is Katie, Meghan, Bridget, Jerry, David, Julia, Kevin, Shannon, Jackie, Ryan and Finally," she said, pointing to each one.

"I'm sorry, did you say 'Finally'?" he said.

Maggi turned Billy aside. "He has six older sisters."

"Oh."

"So, are you ready?"

"I think so, Maggi. Did they meet?"

"I saw the Bishop arrive this morning about nine. He went right into the rectory, and we haven't seen him or Father Bob yet. I can't tell you how nervous I am."

"Me, too. I hope that columnist was right."

Billy gave her hand a squeeze. "I'll see you after mass, Maggi. Bye, kids!"

"Bye, Billy!" They looked at Maggi. "Oooooh!" they teased.

Billy sat back down next to Max and began pointing out the delicate beauty of the church's architecture. Saturday's clouds had given way to rays of sun, which once again filled the worship center with a thousand colors.

Caroline McFarland slowly eased into the first chords of the gathering hymn as the altar servers and the lector took their places in the back of the worship center. From a side room, Bishop Barnes and Father Bob Oliver emerged along with Father Miguel Santos.

As cantor, Maggi announced each hymn.

"Good morning, everyone, and welcome to St. Mary's. Please

join us for our gathering hymn, 'Let Us Build A House,' number 242 in your hymnals. Please stand."

As they stood, Billy looked around at the now-packed church. Many were already wiping their eyes as the Bishop made his way down the aisle behind the procession of the cross. Maggi noticed an empty space in the second row, left side where Grace and Ernie usually sat.

Despite the crowded worship center, the faithful of Logansport sang rather softly that morning. The procession moved seemingly slower than usual, and Patrick Kelly, seated near the back, immediately thought of a funeral.

As they reached the altar, the two servers placed their long candles into holders on either side while a third altar server, carrying a large cross, placed it in a stand directly beneath the large wooden cross suspended from the ceiling.

Bishop Barnes removed the mitre from his head and handed it to Father Santos along with his staff. Father Bob held an open hymnal, but was not singing.

After the last note faded in the vast space, Father Bob stepped slightly forward.

"In the name of the Father, and of the Son, and of the Holy Spirit."

"Amen," the congregation intoned.

"The grace and peace of God our Father and the Lord Jesus Christ be with you always."

"And also with you."

"Heavenly Father, we come before you today as a humbled community. Let us bow our heads and remember our failures. Lord, have mercy."

"Lord, have mercy."

"Christ, have mercy."

"Christ, have mercy."

"Lord, have mercy."

"Lord, have mercy."

Father Bob looked out over the people of St. Mary's. He had promised himself he wouldn't do that until it was absolutely necessary, but within his love for these people, his eyes were drawn to them.

"Glory to God in the highest," he began.

"…and peace to his people on Earth. Lord God, heavenly king…" they continued, reciting the Gloria. He choked back his emotions as even the children joined in.

"…you alone are the most high, Jesus Christ, with the Holy Spirit, in the glory of God the Father. Amen."

Bishop Barnes noticed Father Bob's silence, and motioned for the altar server to bring the book of prayers to him.

"Let us pray. We ask your blessings on the faithful of this flock, to keep them in your heart as you look down upon them. We ask this through our Lord, Jesus Christ…"

"Amen."

With that, the congregation was seated. A middle-aged woman stepped forward to a small lectern to the right of the altar, and opened the lectionary.

"A reading from the book of Chronicles…'The house which I am about to build will be great, for greater is our God than all the gods. But who is able to build a house for Him, for the heavens and the highest heavens cannot contain him?' The word of the Lord."

"Thanks be to God."

As the congregation sang the responsorial Psalm, Bea did her best to explain the different parts of the mass to Billy.

During the last refrain of the Psalm, a last figure found his way to an end pew in the rear of St. Mary's. Karl Schwarz had already loaded his suitcase into the trunk of the Mercedes, and had double-parked in front of the church.

Jimmy Dozan was standing in the back, waiting for this moment. He stepped to the side of the pew where Karl was sitting. Karl finally glanced over, and noticing Jimmy, turned his back on him as best he could in his seat.

This time, a young man stepped to the lectern.

"A reading from the Acts of the Apostles…and Paul said to them 'Be on guard for yourselves and for all the flock, among which the

Holy Spirit has made you overseers, to shepherd the church of God which He purchased with his own blood.' The word of the Lord."

"Thanks be to God."

Father Bob stood and walked to the lectern as the congregation stood for the singing of the Alleluia.

"The Lord be with you," he said.

"And also with you."

"A reading from the holy gospel according to Matthew…'And they went out into the streets, and gathered together all they found, both evil and good; and the wedding hall was filled with dinner guests. But when the king came in to look over the dinner guests, he saw there a man not dressed in wedding clothes, and he said to him, 'Friend, how did you come in here without wedding clothes?' And he was speechless. Then the king said to the servants, 'Bind him hand and foot, and cast him into the outer darkness; in that place there shall be weeping and gnashing of teeth.' For many are called, but few are chosen.' The gospel of the Lord."

"Praise to you Lord Jesus Christ."

The congregation sat down. Father Santos retrieved the Bishop's mitre and placed it on his head. Bishop Barnes stepped slowly to the lectern and looked out over the people of St. Mary's. Not a sound could be heard; Maggi reached under her chair and pulled a tissue from her purse. Patrick Kelly was sitting a few feet away; he caught her eye and gave her a wink.

"My friends," Bishop Barnes began, "for many years this house of the Lord has stood as a testament to your faith. Built by you, cared for by you, it remains a visible reminder that no matter where one finds themselves, they always have a home at St. Mary's.

"However, every home must be able to stand against the forces of time and age. St. Mary's has stood that test admirably.

"As you know, in this day and age the consequences of economics play a greater role in the physical attributes of a church. When those consequences become too great a burden, decisions must be made.

"I was approached several months ago with an offer to ease the burden of those consequences, an offer which I deemed worthwhile."

A few sobs could be heard throughout the church; Karl Schwarz simply smiled.

"And in those months, I have prayed for the direction I and the diocese must take. I know you have prayed as well. It is as a result of these prayers, I believe, that I must read the following letter."

Bishop Barnes unfolded a single piece of paper.

"To the people of Logansport, Illinois. While traveling across the country last summer, I had the occasion to pass within a few miles of your lovely little town. Stopping for the evening, I was afforded the hospitality that is so sorely lacking in my home city. You opened your doors to me without first inquiring of my name or the purpose of my visit.

"In that I had arrived on a weekend, I was able to attend a small gathering of faithful at a mass held in a beautiful park nearby. They gathered in a park because they did not have a building in which to worship, but plans were well under way.

"The pastor of this small flock, Father Birmingham, spoke as eloquently as any I have ever heard in my time. He told his people that with their hard work, and especially their faith, a church will be built on the land where they stood. He also told them that with their faith, the needs for that church shall be met.

"Because of your kindness to a stranger, and your willingness to open your doors to me, I would like to make a small donation to the future building of St. Mary's Church, Logansport, Illinois. In 1893, my company exhibited what was called a stained glass chapel in the Fine Arts Building at the Columbian Exhibition in Chicago. Those windows have remained in storage these past twenty-seven years. As such, I would like to donate them to St. Mary's, so that they will always serve as a reminder to you to keep your doors open to all who wish to enter, friend and stranger alike. Thank you, Logansport, and may God continue to bless each and every one of you."

Bishop Barnes paused and looked at the congregation. Most were looking at the windows, and then back at him.

"The letter is signed 'Louis Comfort Tiffany, March 21, 1920.'"

An audible gasp could be heard throughout the church.

"And as such," he continued, "we are witness not only to a priceless collection of stained glass windows, but more importantly, we are entrusted with a legacy that I am not willing to dispose of. Therefore, I am hereby overriding the diocesan council's decision to close St. Mary's."

Cheers erupted from the people in the church. They stood, hugging each other, crying unashamedly. Max grabbed Billy by the shoulders. "You did it, you beautiful kid you!" Billy smiled, and turned to the choir area. Maggi was hugging Patrick, and the kids were jumping up and down.

Over her father's shoulder, Maggi saw Billy looking at her.

Thank you, she mouthed to him.

Billy gave her a thumbs up, but it wasn't the same as in his days in television. He then patted his chest and pointed at Maggi. "It's all because of you," he said over the cheers.

Not everyone stood to cheer, though.

"NO!"

Karl Schwarz rose slowly from his pew.

"No, no, NO!" he shouted. "We had a deal! WE HAD A DEAL!"

No one listened to him, though. The joyful noise of the faithful drowned him out.

One person did hear him. As Karl pounded his fist on the pew in front of him, Jimmy stepped next to him. He reached into his pocket and pulled out a hundred dollar bill, the same bill he found on his suitcase the night before.

"Here," he said, handing Karl the bill. "I think you're familiar with this process. We'd all appreciate it if you'd leave Logansport. Again."

Karl glared at him, and then down at the money.

"'We,' huh?" he said. He crumpled the bill and dropped it to the floor. "I hope you're all happy together." Karl pushed past Jimmy, walked to the back of the church and disappeared through the large oak doors.

Jimmy took Karl's place in the pew, and setting the kneeler down, knelt with his hands clasped. He looked at each beautiful window in

St. Mary's, taking in each glorious color as if for the first time. He then looked at the cross behind the altar.

"I'm home," he said, and bowed his head.

Chapter 41

"Ernie, you have visitors." Grace patted his hand, and Ernie slowly opened his eyes.

Maggi and Billy stood at the edge of the hospital bed. He looked up at them, and recognized their smiles.

Maggi walked over to the other side and kissed Ernie on the cheek.

"You did it, Ernie. Everything we prayed for, you helped it to happen."

"St. Mary's..." he said.

"Yes, St. Mary's."

Ernie lifted his hand and gently placed it on her cheek.

"You sweet, sweet man. You never doubted, did you?"

"Can't...doubt. No...room."

Maggi took his hand, and kissed his palm. "Please know you're in our prayers, and we want you to get better as quickly as possible."

"Ernie," Grace said, "I hope you don't mind, but I'm going to have young Billy here run things down at the store for a while. I think he's a quick learner."

"Only if you promise to get out of here and be my boss, Ernie," Billy said.

"Okay," Ernie whispered.

Maggi stepped back beside Billy. "We're going to let you rest now," she said.

Ernie pointed at Billy and Maggi.

"You...are...corner...stones," he said.

* * *

"Good afternoon, everyone, it's a glorious fall day here in Logansport, Illinois. I've got a lot of music to get to today, but wanted to just take a moment to thank you for all of your support. Without you, none of this would have been possible. When I came here, you took me in, and made me welcome, and for that, I'll be forever in your debt.

"So let's kick off the show with one of my all-time favorites, Miss Peggy Lee along with Benny Goodman and their classic, 'We'll Meet Again.'

"This is Max Duncan, now and for the foreseeable future, in the afternoon on WLGP AM-610..."

The End

Printed in the United States
28122LVS00002B/94-255